Practical Intelligence for School

~~~~~~~~~~~~~~~~~~~~

Practical Intelligence for School

Wendy M. Williams

Department of Psychology
Yale University

Tina Blythe

Harvard Project Zero

Noel White

Harvard Project Zero

Jin Li

Harvard Project Zero

Robert J. Sternberg

Department of Psychology
Yale University

Howard Gardner

Harvard Project Zero

HarperCollins*CollegePublishers*

Executive Editor: Chris Jennison
Project Coordination, Text and Cover Design: York Production Services
Electronic Production Manager: Mike Kemper
Manufacturing Manager: Helene G. Landers
Electronic Page Makeup: York Production Services
Printer and Binder: R. R. Donnelley & Sons Company
Cover Printer: Phoenix Color Corp.

Funded by a grant from the McDonnell Foundation

Practical Intelligence for School

The order of the first two authors was determined by a coin flip.

Library of Congress Cataloging-in-Publication Data

Practical intelligence for school/Wendy M. Williams...[et al.].
          p.   cm.
     Includes index.
     ISBN 0-673-99850-9
     1. Learning. 2. Thought and thinking. 3. Study Skills. I. Williams, Wendy M. (Wendy Melissa), 1960– .
     LB1060.P68   1996
     370.15'23—dc20   95-24091
                                                                             CIP

95 96 97 98 9 8 7 6 5 4 3 2 1

CONTENTS

Chapter 3

Expository Writing   *44*

Wendy M. Williams and Robert J. Sternberg

Chapter 4

Homework Planning and Execution

Tina Blythe, Noel White, Jin Li, and Howard Gardner

Chapter 5

Preparing for and Using Feedback from Tests

Wendy M. Williams and Robert J. Sternberg

PREFACE

Every year teachers encounter students (sometimes whole rooms full!) who just don't seem to "get" school. Some of these students have trouble finishing their homework or remembering to bring it to school. Some score poorly on tests despite the fact that they seem attentive in class and complete the relevant assignments. Many students simply don't know what to do when they encounter problems as they work—in class and out. Simply put, these students haven't learned how to learn. They are not gaining in *academic* intelligence because they lack *practical* intelligence.

What Is Practical Intelligence?

Practical intelligence is the ability to understand one's environment, and to use this knowledge in figuring out how best to achieve one's goals. There are different (though sometimes overlapping) kinds of practical intelligence for each job or situation we encounter in life. As a teacher, your practical intelligence includes knowing how to meet the administrative demands of the job while conserving enough personal energy to confront the daily challenges of the classroom. Your practical intelligence also includes getting along with colleagues (whether you like them or not), and knowing who can help you secure supplies and other resources. In your life outside of school, practical intelligence involves other kinds of know-how: knowing how to fix your car (or where to get it fixed), how to budget money, how to lift yourself out of a slump, and how to meet emotional needs of friends and family members.

What Is Practical Intelligence for School (PIFS)

To make the most of school and what it has to offer, students, too, need practical intelligence. We call this *Practical Intelligence for School*, or *PIFS*. Through extensive research and practice in a variety of school settings, researchers and teachers have identified five themes as central to students' practical intelligence for school. The themes are phrased in terms of what students need to know.

1. *Knowing Why*

Why does school exist? Why should students learn to read, write, do homework, or take tests? In order to succeed in school, students need to know the purposes of various school tasks, how learning is relevant to their lives now, and how they can use it to improve their lives later.

2. *Knowing Self*

What are the student's personal strengths, weaknesses, habits, and interests? Self-assessment techniques can help students to understand their own work habits and intellectual preferences, and then focus on how to capitalize on strengths and compensate for weaknesses.

3. *Knowing Differences*

How do school subjects differ from one another in content, learning process, and typical testing format? How is studying for a math test, for example, different from studying for social studies? How are the demands of schools similar to, and different from, life outside of school? As students recognize the connections and distinctions among these different kinds of work, they can begin to vary their strategies and working styles appropriately.

4. *Knowing Process*

What should a student do when stuck? What steps (such as making plans and using resources) are involved in completing school tasks? As students focus on process, recognizing and defining problems for themselves, they can plan effective strategies, locate and allocate resources, and use what they know to accomplish their work.

5. *Reworking*

Is the first draft of an assignment the best one? Probably not. Taking time to go over work doesn't always seem worth it, but successful students recognize the importance of self-monitoring and reflection. Reworking pays off.

Why Is It Important to Teach PIFS?

1. PIFS skills are life skills.
2. PIFS skills often are not addressed explicitly in school, even though the most successful students are those who use PIFS skills.
3. More and more students are coming from homes where there is no model for developing these skills.

4. Teachers already have too much to do: Helping students to become more indepen-
    dent learners, to take responsibility for identifying and capitalizing on their
    strengths, can relieve some of this burden.

How Can This Handbook Help?

This handbook provides lessons for developing students' PIFS as they carry out common school tasks. The lessons are not necessarily meant to be followed word for word.
They are presented as models of how to encourage PIFS. The PIFS themes permeate all
of the ideas in this handbook, which is organized into five sections.

An introduction presents the major themes of PIFS and helps students begin the
process of self-evaluation.

Thoughtful Reading covers practical considerations relevant to getting the most
out of reading material from a variety of subject matters.

Expository Writing covers the practical side of creating clear, coherent written
work that best illustrates the student's ideas, talents, and understanding.

Homework Planning and Execution covers the topic of homework and how best
to accomplish it, including how to organize time and materials.

Preparing for and Using Feedback from Tests covers issues relevant to studying
for and taking tests, and ultimately, using the results of tests to the student's advantage.

In Which Subject Areas Can PIFS Be Used?

We designed the PIFS lessons to be used with subjects that are part of all fifth-, sixth-,
and seventh-grade curricula: English, social studies, science, and math. You will find
materials in each of the five sections that are relevant to teaching skills in these subject
areas. Infusing the PIFS lessons into core classes means less time is taken away from
central topics. It also gives you the opportunity to tailor the PIFS approach to the individual needs of your program and students.

How Do I Infuse Practical Intelligence into My Existing Curriculum?

You can use the PIFS curriculum to address specific problems that your students have
encountered. After identifying the problems, browse through the model lessons for
ones that specifically address these issues. Some of the ideas in this handbook are very
concrete (lesson plans that you can follow step-by-step, worksheets, a particular format
for writing assignments). Others are less concrete (discussion questions that you decide
when and how to use). It is up to you and your students to find the ideas that are the
most important for success in your classroom.

You can infuse PIFS ideas into all aspects of your classroom by using the following
questions to examine and revise the assignments you give.

1. Do students have the opportunity to discuss why they are doing this assignment? Will they know how it connects to other things you have done in class? How it connects to their lives outside of school, either now or in the future?
2. Does the assignment give students opportunities to draw on their strengths? Can the assignment be broadened to allow more freedom in how they complete it?
3. Are the steps of the assignment spelled out clearly? Before beginning, do students have a clear picture of what they will need to do to finish? Are they aware of what resources might be useful to them if they encounter a problem?
4. Does the assignment include steps where students reflect on and revise their work? Do they have opportunities to reflect on what they've learned about themselves or the subject matter as they carried it out?

While not every assignment can be reshaped to accommodate all of these concerns, a few of these themes, revisited consistently over the course of several assignments, will foster students' PIFS.

What Is a Workable Implementation Schedule?

During the first month of the school year, you can cover the Introduction to the PIFS Program. Lessons introduce students to two of the five major themes (knowing why and knowing self), and ask students to begin the process of self-evaluation by developing a personal learning profile.

During subsequent months, students work within the four PIFS curriculum sections (Reading, Writing, Homework, and Testing). In addition, each week you can discuss how the PIFS themes intersect with the scholastic curriculum in each subject area, and show how the practical themes are relevant to academic study—of the Civil War, for example, or of fractions.

Lesson selection, sequence, timing, and pace is at your discretion. Once the introduction has been covered, you can skip back and forth among the four focal area booklets. Some lessons can be covered in one or two class periods; others will need more time. You may use the assignments, handouts, and activities suggested in the lessons, or you may develop and revise the materials for your own purposes.

How Is the PIFS Approach Different From Other Study Skills Curricula?

PIFS encompasses some standard study skills but differs from other programs in two important ways. First, instead of offering general solutions, it helps students develop their own approaches to work. Second, rather than being a separate course, the ideas in this handbook are meant to be adapted and used with regular subject matter instruction.

What Does a PIFS Classroom Look Like?

A classroom that fosters students' practical intelligence affords many opportunities for students to learn about themselves and to build on their particular strengths. The assignments usually allow students to draw on different working styles. Project work often plays a prominent role, as well as cooperative learning groups in which students have to depend on the various contributions of different individuals. When a student encounters a problem, she has the opportunity to discuss it with other students, to formulate a solution that she thinks will work for her, to try it out, and to get feedback on the process.

Rather than assigning work or giving rules with no explanation, the teacher in a PIFS classroom is explicit about the purposes for assignments. Students are allowed to discuss their own understanding of these purposes and to try to relate their assignments to the world beyond the classroom and to their current and future lives. As a result of making these connections explicit, students in a PIFS classroom better understand the purposes of their work and are more motivated to pursue it.

In a PIFS classroom, the process is an explicit part of every assignment. Rather than simply telling students to study, the teacher spends time clarifying and modeling what it means to study. Students have opportunities to practice such processes and to reflect on them with other students in class. Use of resources is an important part of assignments and a frequent topic of discussion in PIFS classes. Students learn that they can get help in many different forms and from many different sources. Problems become opportunities to explore new resources and solutions, rather than obstacles to completing the work.

Most important, reflection and reworking are an integral part of every discussion, assignment, and test. PIFS classrooms not only build in time for reflection and feedback, but also provide structure for these activities in the form of worksheets and specific questions to focus reflections and make reflection more useful. Through reflection, students develop more sophisticated understandings of themselves and how they best carry out schoolwork.

What would you see if you observed a PIFS classroom in action? Students would be presenting projects showing their special talents and abilities in areas not usually focused on in school projects: writing songs, designing costumes, demonstrating gymnastics, preparing recipes, acting out skits, and so on. Students would be sharing their unique skills and strengths and developing an understanding of how they can contribute to classwork in an original way. Instead of approaching them with dread, students would be excited about home writing assignments and project work because they would have a more active role in choosing their topics and planning how to accomplish their assignments.

You would also see students using specific strategies to help them do homework and prepare for tests, so that their performance matched their teacher's expectations. Students would be reading "smart"—reading some things more carefully than others, and focusing on the most important sections of everything they read. They would also be writing smart by using various processes to make their compositions creative and interesting to teachers. All in all, what you would see in a PIFS classroom is students *engaged* in learning because they have the necessary skills to guide their academic progress—students who *know how to learn*.

How Do I Know PIFS Is Working?

To evaluate the curriculum and its impact on students, several types of assessments are incorporated into the curriculum. Teachers can grade students' PIFS worksheets and projects if they wish, or evaluate students' work in any subject area to see if PIFS skills are catching on. The PIFS curriculum also asks students to keep a PIFS journal over the school year. This journal can provide insight into the development of students' PIFS skills. But the best way to know if PIFS is working is to watch for the signs that the classroom environment is being transformed into the type of classroom just described. The teacher will know without a doubt that PIFS is working when all students make good use of their skills and strengths to perform effectively within the school environment. PIFS doesn't mean every child will get an A, but it does mean that every child will make an effort and do her or his best.

What Is the Student with Practical Intelligence Like?

Students with practical intelligence for school understand why they are attending school and see the benefits school confers. They see the relationships between schoolwork and life outside of school, between performance now and success later. Although they may not like homework and tests, they understand why they are required to complete them.

They are active learners who make full use of their unique complement of intellectual skills. They know how to capitalize on strengths and compensate for weaknesses as they confront tasks in these domains.

Students with practical intelligence know how to evaluate their own work and the work of others. They utilize feedback from teachers, parents, and peers to best advantage. Perhaps most important, these students know how to recognize and solve problems, whether they exist in a textbook or in the less clearly defined world outside of the classroom.

What Are the Principles Underlying PIFS?

Now that you are somewhat familiar with the organization and content of PIFS, you may be wondering why, exactly, the curriculum was developed. Where did the ideas for PIFS come from, and why does it work?

The concepts on which PIFS is based are concerned with precisely what is meant by the term *intelligence*. What is intelligence, really? In school, intelligence is usually defined and assessed by tests of verbal and mathematical reasoning ability. But this conception of intelligence is very limited.

In the real world, intelligence means much more than good test grades—it includes understanding oneself and knowing how to make oneself happy, getting along with others, and solving real-world problems. Intelligence includes artistic and musical abilities, knowing how to read and work with people in different situations, and knowing how to make a meal or fix a leaky roof. It also includes athletic ability, such as being a good dancer or basketball player. In fact, intelligence encompasses many aspects of lifelong functioning. Being good at tests is one part of being intelligent, but it is certainly not the only important part.

The recognition that intelligence is a far broader concept than had previously been recognized led two researchers to explore the full domain of human intellectual ability. Working independently, Robert J. Sternberg of Yale University and Howard Gardner of Harvard University developed theories of human intelligence based on a comprehensive assessment of intellectual ability and functioning. The desire to collaborate on curricula that would enhance all types of intelligence in school children led these researchers and their associates to develop PIFS.

Through PIFS, students learn to recognize and develop the different aspects of their own intelligence. They also learn how to enhance and apply dimensions of their practical intelligence in order to get the most out of school. The curriculum encourages students to conceptualize intelligence as a broad set of abilities, and to be proud of their own complement of these abilities while respecting the abilities of their peers. Overall, PIFS emphasizes *life skills* that relate intelligence to the real world in which the student must function, whether it is the world of school or the world outside of school.

How Was PIFS Developed and Tested?

The PIFS Project was a collaboration by researchers from Yale and Harvard Universities, funded by The James S. McDonnell Foundation of St. Louis, Missouri. Over a six-year period several versions of the PIFS curriculum were developed, first by Harvard and Yale researchers working separately and then by the two research teams in collaboration. Contributors to the earlier versions of the practical intelligence curriculum included Mara Krechevsky and Joan Makepeace at Harvard and Lynn Okagaki and Alice Jackson at Yale.

As the practical intelligence curriculum was developed, several versions of the curriculum were evaluated in multiple trials in an extensive research program conducted in 11 schools in Massachusetts and 5 schools in Connecticut. The evaluation of PIFS compared school-year performance gains for students in PIFS classrooms with performance gains for students from the same and nearby schools *not* receiving PIFS. The data gathered were voluminous and we can only summarize them here. In every evaluation, students receiving PIFS instruction showed significantly greater gains over the school year compared to students not receiving PIFS.

For example, in one evaluation PIFS students scored greater gains on the Survey of Study Habits and Attitudes (Brown & Holtzman, 1967) and the Learning and Study Skills Inventory (Weinstein & Palmer, 1988). In a later implementation, the researchers developed customized assessments measuring students' academic and practical abilities in reading, writing, homework, and test-taking. (For example, academic writing ability means being able to write a grammatically correct essay with good organization, spelling, punctuation, and so on. Practical writing ability means being able to write a composition that is persuasive, interesting, and appropriate for the audience.) PIFS students performed significantly better than control students on assessments in all four of these areas in both the academic and practical domains. PIFS students also were rated easier to manage in the classroom and more apt to display active-learning skills, among other important behaviors. Data on student performance and teacher reactions to PIFS were used to improve the curriculum. This handbook represents the culmination of our six-year program of research. *The goal of the PIFS handbook is to help you shape a classroom and a curriculum that gives all students the opportunity to develop their practical intelligence.*

ACKNOWLEDGMENTS

We would like to acknowledge the invaluable contributions of the many people who supported the Practical Intelligence for School Project. In particular, we would like to thank the teachers who worked most closely with us in the development, implementation, and assessment of the Practical Intelligence for School curriculum. They gave generously of their expertise and time. Without their help, this project would not have been possible:

William Allen, Wamogo Regional School District, CT
Toby Caplin, Graham and Parks Elementary School, Cambridge, MA
Robert Duke, Wamogo Regional School District, CT
Janis Edwards, Curley Middle School, Boston, MA
Barbara Fox, Martin Luther King, Jr. Middle School, Cambridge, MA
Mary Goullaud, Healey Elementary School, Somerville, MA
Ellen Hill, Curley Middle School, Boston, MA
Dan Klemmer, Graham and Parks Elementary School, Cambridge, MA
Michelle Pratt, Wamogo Regional School District, CT
Voncille Ross, Curley Middle School, Boston, MA
Nancy Waltonen, Curley Middle School, Boston, MA
Guy Weik, Wamogo Regional School District, CT

We are also grateful to those teachers and administrators who provided us with advice, suggestions, and opportunities to test versions of the curriculum and the assessment instruments:

Janice Abbruzzi, Watertown Middle School, Watertown, MA
Mary Balasalle, Lewis Middle School, Boston, MA
Anne Barysh, Pierce Elementary School, Brookline, MA
Robert Bates, Heath Elementary School, Brookline, MA
Marcia Baynes, Longfellow Elementary School, Cambridge, MA
Ed Belliveau, Pierce Elementary School, Brookline, MA
Timothy Breslin, Wamogo Regional School District, CT
Eileen Carroll, Agassiz Elementary School, Cambridge, MA
Debra Collins, O'Maley Middle School, Gloucester, MA

Caroline Connolly, Pierce Elementary School, Brookline, MA
Sheila Corbin, Curley Middle School, Boston, MA
Ron Cutraro, Heath Elementary School, Brookline, MA
Marcia DeFelice, O'Maley Middle School, Gloucester, MA
Brenda Flood, Curley Middle School, Boston, MA
Margaret Giacoppo, Agassiz Elementary School, Cambridge, MA
Elizabeth Grace, O'Maley Middle School, Gloucester, MA
Sandra Hegstad, Heath Elementary School, Brookline, MA
Sandra Hilly, Curley Middle School, Boston, MA
Sheila Ketlack-Grice, Curley Middle School, Boston, MA
Joan Krevy, Watertown Middle School, Watertown, MA
Richard Kleponis, Chenery Middle School, Belmont, MA
Kathleen M. Love, O'Maley Middle School, Gloucester, MA
Helen Maloney, Healey Elementary School, Somerville, MA
Marilyn Mazer, Chenery Middle School, Belmont, MA
Debbie Mercer, Runkle Elementary School, Brookline, MA
Thomas Misuraco, O'Maley Middle School, Gloucester, MA
Mary Ellen Moore, O'Maley Middle School, Gloucester, MA
Clare Moss, Chenery Middle School, Belmont, MA
Arlene O'Neil, O'Maley Middle School, Gloucester, MA
Ann Marie Patten, O'Maley Middle School, Gloucester, MA
Mary Rudolf, O'Maley Middle School, Gloucester, MA
Robin Welch, Runkle Elementary School, Brookline, MA
Judy Zimmerman, Watertown Middle School, Watertown, MA

We would also like to thank the entire administration, faculty, and staff of Lynn Middle School in Tewksbury, MA. Their adoption of and feedback about the PIFS Curriculum provided us with many useful ideas for improving it.

Special thanks to our fellow researchers who worked on earlier phases of the PIFS Project:

Thomas Hatch, Harvard Project Zero
Alice Jackson, Yale University
Mara Krechevsky, Harvard Project Zero
Joan Makepeace, Harvard Project Zero
Lenora Manzelli, Yale University
Lynn Okagaki, Yale University
Gregg Solomon, Harvard Project Zero

Finally, we wish to express our appreciation to the James S. McDonnell Foundation for its generous funding of this project.

CHAPTER 1

Introduction to the Practical Intelligence for School Program

Noel White, Tina Blythe, Jin Li, and Howard Gardner

Contents

About the Introduction Chapter

As with much of the Practical Intelligence for School (PIFS) curriculum, the ideas in this section can be used at any time during the year and can be repeated frequently. It is an "introduction" because the lessons raise for students some of the key questions and important attitudes that you will find throughout the other sections.

Why Go to School?

One of the main questions that PIFS asks of students is "Why?" In the first lesson, students are asked to think about the nature of school and why they attend. In the other sections, students consider the purposes of reading and writing, why they do homework, and why tests are important. Students often do *not* ask why they do things, but simply continue doing the work because "they have to." The PIFS lessons should help to motivate students and help them to see how school activities can be useful in their lives both now and in the future.

What Is Intelligence?

One of the main goals of the PIFS program is to move students away from common misconceptions about intelligence, and toward more productive attitudes.

Common Misconceptions	More Useful Conceptions
• Intelligence is a fixed thing that you either have or don't have.	• Intelligence is something that you can improve through work, thinking about yourself, and monitoring your actions.
• There is only one kind of intelligence—everyone who's smart is smart in the same way.	• There are many different ways to be intelligent—everyone is smart in some ways and not so smart in others.

Although it can take a long time to change someone's attitude about intelligence, the lessons in this section start to raise important questions and to suggest the variety of ways that people can be talented.

How Am I Intelligent?

As students get older, they have to take more and more responsibility for their own learning. The lessons in this section help students start to think about how they may need to concentrate more on some areas than others. Throughout the PIFS program, students should draw on this idea by learning to personalize school experiences given their own interests and unique ways of learning.

How Do I Know That I Am Improving?

In the following lessons, and throughout the PIFS curriculum, students focus on themselves and reflect on the nature of the work that they do in school. Their experiences and thoughts can be forgotten easily unless there are ways for them to keep track of what they learn. A journal can serve this purpose by providing a place for students to record significant accomplishments, important moments, and new ideas.

You and your students decide how best to use a journal. For example, you might leave it up to students to determine what and when they write in their journals, or you might give more structure to their writing by assigning particular topics or times to write. In place of a journal, you might want to videotape or audiotape particular discussions, presentations, or student work.

In any case, encourage students to focus on *process*—how they learn and improve, become organized, or become better writers—in order to avoid the idea that they have unchangeable traits. Be sure to provide opportunities for students to review what they've done, to return later to some of the questions raised early in the year, and to recognize the progress they make.

LESSON 1.1 Why School?

Synopsis

A brief discussion to raise some of the kinds of questions that will be an important part of the Practical Intelligence for School program throughout the year.

What To Do

1. Give students a chance to think individually about why they go to school. You might use one or two of the questions listed for discussion below. You might have students write in journals as homework or for five minutes before starting discussion. Or you might have them simply take a minute to think quietly before starting the discussion.

2. Lead a group discussion based on broad questions that students can answer from their own experience, such as:

    - What is school?
    - What would you be doing if you weren't attending school?
    - Why do you think schools were started in the first place?
    - Most children used to start work on farms or in factories at a very young age. What do you think those children missed by not going to school?
    - In what ways might it be better *not* to have school?
    - What kinds of things do you learn in school?
    - What makes an excellent school?
    - What do you need to know to do well in school?
    - How does school prepare you for later life?
    - What do you need to know to help you outside of school and later in life?

    There is no need to cover all questions.

3. Tell students that these are the kinds of questions that the class will be considering through the year. You might want to use the metaphor of "looking behind the scenes." Through PIFS, the class will learn about what is behind school success and will develop skills for making school a better experience. These skills are also essential *outside* of school, and in later life as well.

Connections

Homework Lesson 4.1: Purposes for Homework

Testing Lesson 5.1: Why Tests?

Follow-Up Activity

Whenever students start a new activity or project, have them think about *why* they are being asked to do it. How does it fit in with other things they do for school? What might they learn? How is it like what people do outside of school?

LESSON 1.2 **Redefining Intelligence**

Synopsis

Introductory discussion and brainstorming about notions of intelligence.

What To Do

1. Introduce the importance of thinking about intelligence. One possible way:

    - Part of your (the students') job this year will be to show me (the teacher) how you are smart.
    - This job will be easy because each of you already is smart in many different ways.
    - This job won't be so easy because you may not know *how* you are smart, how to *demonstrate* your abilities, or how to *develop* them.
    - Part of my job is to help you figure out your strengths and how to use them.
    - A good place to start is to think about what "smart" (or "intelligent") means. Our own personal definitions of intelligence can influence how we think of ourselves and what we do—both in and out of school.

2. Give students a chance to think individually about intelligence by writing in journals or simply having a moment to think quietly before class discussion.

3. For a class discussion, ask students to describe particular people that they think are very good at something. If they have trouble, you might ask them to think of relatives, friends, famous people, heroes—people whom they would want to be.

4. Encourage diverse examples. If students focus mainly on academic talent, ask them to think of talented musicians, athletes, artists, actors, cooks, auto mechanics, and so on. Continuing for about 10 minutes, ask students to talk about how each person is talented. What kind of intelligence does that person need to do what she does so well? What special talent does he have? You might keep track of the range of responses on a board.

5. Review their ideas and have the class think about what it means to be intelligent.

6. Encourage the notion that intelligence is an ability to do things that we value and that there are many different ways to be productive and talented. Also encourage the notion that people's abilities change and *improve* over time.

    - Can you think of people who are smart at one thing, and terrible at another?
    - Can you remember when you couldn't do something that you're very good at now?
    - If someone does well in school, will she be able to do well in *anything*?

7. Sum up what the class has said. Inform students that they will spend much of the year thinking about their own talents and improving how they work in school. Use this opportunity to define PIFS for students, if you haven't already done so. Let them know that PIFS will involve recognizing their own strengths and interests and then using those strengths to make school more meaningful and interesting.

Connections

Introduction Lesson 1.3: Sharing Talents

Introduction Lesson 1.4: Puzzle Challenges

Follow-Up Activity

See Follow-Up Activities 2 and 3 for the next lesson (Lesson 3).

LESSON 1.3 **Sharing Talents**

Synopsis

Students reflect on past experiences—activities, projects, hobbies—that indicate talents and/or interests.

What To Do

1. Several days before you plan to take a class period for this lesson, ask students to think about things they like to do and things they have done well in or out of school. Encourage students to think of a wide range of things. For example, handling interpersonal relations well—such as showing kindness or consideration for someone else—is a special talent.

2. Have students spend some time at home preparing to demonstrate a talent or something that they have done well. Encourage them to work with family members or friends to prepare.

3. Try to avoid having students simply talk when they share their talents with the class. You might require that each student bring concrete evidence of the talent, or that (if possible) they directly demonstrate what they can do. Some possible ways that students can share their talents include: re-enacting a significant event, showing something the student built, singing, performing a brief dance, displaying a drawing or painting, making a chart or diagram of progress in some area.

4. On the day when students present to the class, some of them may be embarrassed at having to reveal something about themselves in front of everyone else. To help these students, you might emphasize that the presentation itself is not so important as *learning something about themselves*, and learning more about the diversity of talents that people have. You might allow them to work with just a few other students in small groups; or, if possible, allow them to present this assignment individually after school or during a free period. Another alternative is to pair students and have them learn something about their partners to recount to the rest of the class.

5. Allow other students to ask questions of each presenter. Be sure to ask students to recall when they were less good, when they could *not* have demonstrated whatever skills they have now. What did they do to improve? How have they learned what they now know? Some questions for general discussion include: Why do we have favorite subjects and activities? Why do we have weak areas, or areas in which we don't do as well?

6. If time permits, summarize (or have students summarize) the range of talents represented in your class.

Connections

Introduction Lesson 1.2: Redefining Intelligence

Homework Lesson 4.6: Making It More Interesting and Personal

Writing Lesson 3.3: Getting Down to Work

Follow-Up Activities

1. To begin tying students' extracurricular strengths to the skills they need in school, ask them to write in journals about their greatest in-school strength. Then ask them to describe how that strength is similar to, or different from, the talent they demonstrated for the class.

2. Have every student create a personal coat of arms that shows a favorite out-of-school activity, a favorite school subject, the skill or activity desired to improve outside school, and the school subject or skill desired to improve. (This activity also could be used *in place of* the suggestions under step 3 above.)

3. Periodically ask students to nominate classmates for an award recognizing nonacademic skills such as heading off a potential fight or fixing something in the classroom that had broken. After collecting nominations, have every student select one of the nominees, then write a paragraph about why she or he respects this person, giving specific reasons why the person deserves the award. Select a winner based on what students write, making sure that every student wins at some point in the year.

LESSON 1.4 Puzzle Challenges

Synopsis

Activities for students to overcome challenges and to exercise different abilities.

What To Do

1. This lesson will take some planning time to determine what puzzles and challenges to give students, and then about two periods of class time: one for the challenging tasks, and the other for a follow-up discussion.

2. As a class, brainstorm ideas for simple activities or tasks that will challenge students. These challenges should be chosen or designed to demonstrate two things:

    • It is often possible to overcome tasks that may appear difficult or impossible.
    • There are many different ways to solve a problem or to handle a single task.

3. If you prefer, skip the brainstorming and simply use the Problem-Solving Tasks described at the end of this lesson. Or, the suggestions can be used as examples to start your class thinking about other puzzles, games, and challenges.

4. Set up the materials or instructions around the room for the activities that you or your class decides to try.

5. Remind students that they have been thinking about what they are good at and about how they may work differently from other students. Let them know that today's activities should be fun, but that they should think about how each person works in a unique way, and how it is often possible to overcome tasks that appear challenging.

6. Ask them to try as many of the tasks as they can. Encourage students to try challenging ones even if they might be hesitant or think they won't do well.

7. Follow up the puzzles and tasks with discussion, either immediately after or on the next day. Ask students to describe what they liked and disliked, why, what they did to solve each puzzle or to do each task, what was difficult, how they dealt with difficulty, and how they felt (proud, excited, anxious). Emphasize the different ways that different students approached the same challenges.

8. Point out that many school tasks—writing papers, taking tests, doing projects—are similar, in that each student has to find his or her own way of handling the work; and what may at first appear difficult often *can* be done with hard work, creativity,

and patience. Ask students to talk about school assignments that they have found difficult but have been able to do.

Problem-Solving Tasks

Representing Rhythm

Represent the rhythm of any familiar, simple tune with something physical such as blocks or Cuisennaire™ rods.

Describing an Arrangement of Objects

Describe how a group of objects is arranged so that a second person who has a set of the same objects can duplicate the arrangement without actually seeing the original one. This can be done by having two people sit facing each other, each with a matching group of objects (one arranged, the other not), but with a barrier between them.

Describing the School

Describe the physical structure of your school so that someone who has never been there will know as much about it as possible. The description need not be in words; students may use drawings, models, or whatever is appropriate.

Jumping Pegs

Use a board with a pattern (usually a triangle or a cross) of holes in it. Fill the holes with pegs, leaving only one empty. Remove pegs from the board by "jumping" a peg from one hole over an adjacent peg and into an empty hole. The peg that is jumped over is removed from the board. When only one peg is left on the board, or the remaining pegs are spaced such that no more jumping can occur, count how many pegs are left. The object is to end up with as few pegs as possible left on the board.

Drawing

Draw a few simple objects such as a glue bottle, a glass, a chair, or an earring. Try drawing each object more than once, drawing it in a different way each time.

Naming States

List all of the states you can remember in one minute without looking at a map or anyone else's list. How did you generate your list? Did you picture the states in your head, draw a map, list them alphabetically, think of the states nearest to home or the ones you've visited? Or did you use some other method?

Puzzling Words

Solve word puzzles, such as "wordles," where a very simple drawing stands for a common phrase or word.

Figuring How Parts Fit Together

Take apart and then reassemble a small mechanical object, such as a hand-held oil pump or a kitchen meat grinder (*not* an electrical one).

Connections

Introduction Lesson 1.2: Redefining Intelligence

Homework Lesson 4.2: Knowing Your Personal Needs

Testing Lesson 5.5: Understanding Your Memory

Testing Lesson 5.6: Understanding Test Questions

Follow-Up Activity

Whenever you notice different students taking different approaches to accomplish a task (such as doing a school project or convincing classmates to start up a game on the playground), point out how their approaches differ even though each accomplishes something worthwhile. Is one approach better than the other? Why do we sometimes do things so differently from each other? Would a student gain anything from trying a different approach than what comes naturally?

LESSON 1.5 Individual Differences in School

Synopsis

A brainstorm/discussion and a writing task to help students think about the purpose of school and how they fit into the bigger picture of school.

What To Do

1. Refer students to the previous lessons and ask them to recall what they learned about themselves. Briefly discuss the variety of talents and approaches that these activities revealed. How many people did *not* have the same interests? How many people did *not* do a particular task in the same way?

2. Have the class consider some of the demands that school makes on students. *If we're all so different, why do we go to the same school and do almost everything in the same way?* Brainstorm ideas. Keep track of students' answers for everyone to see. Ideas might include the need for common skills and shared knowledge, as well as the necessity of having a practical way of educating a lot of students at once.

3. Acknowledge the importance of reasons that students name: Everyone *should* learn how to read and write, and *should* be able to get a job, and *is* bound by law to attend school. But that doesn't change the fact that we are all different and react to things in different ways.

4. Ask students to think about a time when they were asked to do something that they knew they didn't do very well or didn't like very much but had to do it anyway. You might want to have students write about their thoughts in journals, or as a class assignment.

5. Summarize (or have students summarize) what they discussed during this lesson.

6. This would be another good opportunity to describe the purpose of PIFS if you haven't done so. PIFS will help students to work on the kinds of problems raised in this lesson by learning about themselves, taking more control of their school experiences, learning to handle work that is difficult, building on their individual abilities, tailoring school assignments to fit their interests, and pursuing tasks from different angles.

Connections

Homework Lesson 4.3: Personal Solutions to Homework Difficulties

Homework Lesson 4.6: Making It More Interesting and Personal

Writing Lesson 3.3: Getting Down to Work

Follow-Up Activity

Any time that your students are unusually frustrated or intimidated by something that you've assigned, you might refer them back to this lesson or to their journal notes from this lesson. Have their reactions to school changed over time? If so, why? Are they getting any better at handling things that they don't necessarily like to do? If not, what can they do to improve the situation?

CHAPTER 2

Thoughtful Reading

Tina Blythe, Noel Wite, Jin Li, and Howard Gardner

Contents

Reading Themes

1. Knowing Why
   - What are the purposes of reading, in *and* out of school?
   - How is reading more, or less, effective than other ways of getting information?
2. Knowing Differences
   - Understanding the different kinds of written material, their differing purposes, and knowing different reading approaches that are appropriate for each.
3. Knowing Self
   - Recognizing current reading patterns and preferences.
   - Identifying personal strengths and weaknesses in terms of reading.
4. Knowing Process
   - Knowing strategies for reading actively.
   - Knowing how to get unstuck.
5. Re-Reading
   - Understanding the purpose of re-reading.
   - Developing strategies for re-reading effectively.

About the Reading Chapter

Reading is perhaps the most important skill that students acquire in school—and the most misunderstood. Though many students learn to decode words adequately, few of them recognize the complex and variable applications that make reading a truly useful tool. The lessons in this section help students to appreciate the importance of reading in school and out, to broaden their conceptions of the various kinds and purposes of reading, and to help them acquire the specific strategies they need to become more effective readers.

The Five Themes

Lesson 1 emphasizes "knowing why" and "knowing self."

Lesson 2 emphasizes "knowing differences" and "knowing process."

Lesson 3 emphasizes "knowing self" and "knowing process."

Lesson 4 emphasizes "knowing process" and "knowing differences."

Lesson 5 emphasizes "knowing process."

Lesson 6 emphasizes "re-reading."

Overview of the Lessons

In **Lesson 1**, students relate school reading tasks to the reading they do in their out-of-school lives and to the reading that adults do in their careers.

Reading is not a static skill, but one which students must adapt to various kinds of reading material. **Lesson 2** helps students to recognize the variations in purpose, content, and format of what they read and to choose strategies appropriate to the task.

Lesson 3 helps students to consider and plan for the many other factors that influence the quality of their reading: individual preferences, attitude, work place, other activities that compete for time and attention, the difficulty of the material. Because these factors vary from task to task as well as from person to person, this lesson engages students in evaluating these issues for themselves and in developing personal reading plans that take them into account.

Lesson 4 focuses on expanding students' repertoire of specific techniques on which they can draw to solve particular problems.

For middle school students, the confusion and frustration that come from trying to read challenging material can lead them simply to quit trying to make sense of it. **Lesson 5** offers specific problem-solving strategies to which students can resort in times of trouble.

Lesson 6 addresses re-reading, a particularly difficult strategy for young students. It gives students the opportunity to discuss the value of re-reading and it presents some specific strategies for making re-reading more useful.

LESSON 2.1 Why Read?

Central Themes

Knowing Why

Knowing Self

Synopsis

A "reading inventory" and a discussion to help students think about the role that reading plays in their everyday lives and in the lives of adults.

What To Do

1. Ask students how much time they spend reading each day. Probably they'll tell you "Not very much." But don't take their word for it. Ask questions about their television watching: Do they read the credits at the beginning and end of shows (what Bart Simpson writes on the chalkboard, for example)? Do they read the slogans that flash on the screen during commercials ("Just do it" at the end of the Nike commercials)? How about the comics, or the headlines in the newspaper that someone left on the bus seat next to them, or the sign on the front of the bus telling its destination? Continue to brainstorm with students for a few minutes until they seem to understand that everything counts—the backs of cereal boxes, the jacket of a new tape or CD, the billboards on the street, TV Guide—everything. (This list and other lists brainstormed in the lesson will be used in later lessons, so they should be recorded in a way that can easily be reproduced for the class. A flip pad of large sheets that can be posted on the walls of the classroom might be helpful.)

2. Now challenge them to keep track for one day (from one class period to the same class period the next day) of all the times they read *anything*. (You might set up a little competition by inviting other classes to carry out the same activity and then comparing whole-class totals the next day.) Students can keep a running tally on small pieces of paper or index cards.

3. Begin the next class by asking all students for their totals (this can be done anonymously if you prefer). Add them all up and write the grand total on the board. Then stand back and admire it with everyone. Discuss with students the following:

    *   Did they find themselves reading things that they hadn't listed in yesterday's brainstorm?
    *   Why do they think there are so many things that need to be read?
    *   What are the advantages and disadvantages of getting information through reading (as opposed to television or radio or other nonprint sources)?

- What would their lives be like if they couldn't read?
- What would the world be like if there were no such thing as reading or writing?

4. Help students to think about the role that reading plays in adult life by doing one or more of the following activities:

   - If possible, invite community members to your class to talk about when reading is useful to them in their jobs (a volunteer from a literacy program is a possibility).
   - Alternatively, the students could write letters to celebrities as well as local people to ask about their reading habits. (A similar activity is proposed in the writing section, so students might write a single letter asking both questions.)
   - Or, students might simply suggest particular jobs and list the sorts of reading those jobs might entail.

5. Next, help students think about how the reading they do in school compares to the kinds of reading they (and adults) do outside of school. Have students list the different kinds of reading they do in school (encourage them to think about *all* subjects, including math) and how this reading differs from the reading they do out of school. Probe their responses—even the simple and superficial ones. If, for example, students claim that the reading they do in school is boring and pointless, ask them to make some guesses about why it is assigned. Ask them to compare their school assignments with some of the reading examples that they tallied, as well as with the types of reading adults say they do for their jobs. Which kinds of reading are most similar to their school reading? You might also ask them what in general would make school reading more tolerable for them, as well as what they themselves might do to make it better. (Lesson 3 takes up this point more fully.)

Connections

Introduction Lesson 1.1: Why School?

Writing Lesson 3.1: Writing In School and Out

Follow-Up Activities

1. Ask students to survey people in their community (storekeepers, police officers, teachers, parents, siblings) about what they read and why. Each week, ask two or three students to interview one person each. At the end of the week, they can report their findings, which can be recorded in a public place in the classroom.

2. If you teach in a self-contained classroom, take a few minutes each week to discuss reading in one subject other than language arts. Invite students to make connections and find differences in the purposes for reading in their various subjects.

LESSON 2.2 Differences in Kinds of Reading and Reading Strategies

Central Themes

Knowing Differences

Knowing Process

Synopsis

A comparison/contrast exercise to help students recognize different kinds of reading and the different reading strategies they necessitate.

What To Do

1. Prepare a handout that reproduces three short passages of familiar kinds of reading matter. Likely candidates: a selection from a science or social studies text, another from a newspaper, and a third from a piece of fiction. The pieces should be unlabelled so that students can't tell their sources.

2. Present students with the handout and read aloud each selection with them. Explain to the students that they need to figure out the source of each piece by examining it very closely and looking for clues that might "give away" its identity.

3. Before students begin making guesses, you might want to discuss how the selections are the same and how they are different. When they're ready to start assigning identities to the passages, keep track of their suggestions on the board. Ask each student for some piece of evidence that indicates that one passage is probably from a textbook while another seems more likely to be from a newspaper or a story. Encourage students to pay attention to things like subheadings, descriptions, dates, passages in quotation marks, and so forth. You should wind up with several lists on the board, each headed with the name of a particular kind of reading and comprised of a list of characteristics that typlify it.

4. Unveil the true sources for the students and let them see how well they did.

5. Having demonstrated that there are different kinds of reading materials, you can now help students think about the different strategies that each kind of reading material requires. Ask students why they read social studies textbooks. Most of the answers will probably revolve around school ("because I have to for homework" or "because I'll have to take a test on it"). Next, ask them why they read the newspaper, and the answers will probably be quite different ("because I want to see who won the game" or "because I like reading the comics" or "because I was interested in the picture on the front page").

6. Given these different purposes, question them about *how* they read these two pieces.

    •   Do they read the textbook and the newspaper in the same way? (If many students respond yes to this question, ask them why again. It is crucial here for them to see that reading—like speaking and writing and cooking and almost any other daily task they can think of—can be done for different purposes and that each purpose involves different approaches.)
    •   How do they read when they have to study for a test? (Quickly or slowly? Once or several times? Taking notes? Reading captions/summaries?) If students don't give good responses based on their experience, ask them to imagine what else they might do if they wanted to do really well on the test.
    •   How do they read the newspaper when they want to find a piece of information quickly? (By skimming or by reading everything carefully?)
    •   How does reading a short story differ from either of those situations?
    •   What would happen if they tried to read the newspaper in the same way they read their social studies text? Or a short story?

During this discussion, emphasize to students the need to think carefully about *why* they are reading something before they begin reading it, and to choose appropriate ways of reading for that purpose. Point out that, as they get older, there will be more and more demands on their time—more school work, more after-school activities, more people with whom they want to spend time. (Maybe they're already feeling a little of this pressure now, on nights when they have homework in two subjects *and* want to go to the movies with their friends.) If they learn how to choose reading strategies according to the purpose of the reading, they can save themselves a lot of time.

For example, if they want to find out the score of last night's game, it would be pointless to read every article in the entire paper. Instead, they would turn to the sports section and skim headlines until they saw "Bulls Trample Celtics." Then they would skim the article until the numbers "103–89" caught their eye. Similarly, if they were looking for specific information in a social studies or science text, or if they were reviewing certain information for at test, they might skim titles and subheadings until they saw something that looked relevant, and then read more carefully to find the exact information. However, if they were reading because they were taking notes for a report, they would probably read more carefully, making sure they understood all the information, so as to decide what to include in their notes.

Ultimately, students should know that understanding *what kind of reading* they are doing and *why* they are doing it are important first steps in reading well.

Connections

Writing Lesson 3.6: A Revision Process (particularly the section about the importance of revising for a particular purpose)

Follow-Up Activity

Each time you assign reading, let your students know what you want them to get out of it: perhaps preparation for a class discussion the next day, or for the test next week, or background information for a report they will have to do. This sense of purpose will enable students to choose their reading strategies more effectively.

LESSON 2.3 **Personal Reading Profiles**

Central Themes

Knowing Self

Knowing Process

Synopsis

Journal writing and discussion to help students reflect on their current reading practices and preferences and begin to use this information to read more effectively.

What To Do

1. Prepare copies of four handouts (included in the Student Handout section at the end this chapter):

    • "Geraldo's Reading: A Practice Case"
    • "Geraldo's Reading Plan" worksheet
    • "Personal Reading Plan" worksheet
    • "Evaluation of Personal Reading Plan" worksheet

2. Have students return to the list of reading activities (both in school and out) that they brainstormed in Lesson 1. Allow them to add anything important that they left out the first time.

3. Ask them to write in their journals the answers to the following questions:

    • What kind of reading do you like the most?
    • What is the easiest or most enjoyable thing about that kind of reading?
    • What kind of reading do you like the least?
    • What is the hardest or least enjoyable thing about that kind of reading?
    • When and where do you do your best reading?
    • What circumstances make it hard for you to read?

4. Have students briefly share their answers to these questions. On the board, make notes of trends as well as significant differences in their answers. When they've finished, point out to students the variations in what they like to read, what makes reading hard, and how they like to do it. Acknowledge that reading can be a difficult and complicated process—especially when it is not done for pleasure. However, students can take steps to make reading easier for themselves.

5. Tell students that one way to make hard reading easier is to develop a personal reading plan. These personal reading plans should take into account how they work best and what they like and dislike about their reading assignments. Distribute copies of "Geraldo's Reading: A Practice Case" (at the end of this chapter) and read it aloud with the students.

Geraldo's Reading: A Practice Case

Directions

READ the information on this page about Geraldo's homework and his reading profile.

DECIDE the best way for Geraldo to do his science reading, as well as the rest of his homework.

Geraldo's Homework

- Read Chapter 7 (five pages long) in his science book and answer the ten questions at the end of the chapter
- Solve 20 math problems
- Do a short worksheet on verbs for language arts

Geraldo's Reading Profile

- He *hates* science reading because
    1. it is hard to understand;
    2. it takes him a long time to complete.
- He likes math homework the best because it doesn't involve any reading.
- When he tries to read, the television set often distracts him—but his favorite show comes on right after school.
- He can't really concentrate on difficult reading for more than 15 minutes at a time.
- He's usually tired and in a bad mood when he gets home from school.

---

6. After the class has read it once, talk briefly with the students about these questions:

    - Given his mood, what should Geraldo do first? Why?
    - Given the rest of his homework, what should Geraldo do first, second, etc.? Why?
    - What can he do about the fact that he can't concentrate on hard reading for long?
    - Where should he work? Why?
    - What can he do to make the science reading easier to understand?

    (Troubleshooting strategies like the ones students talk about here will be covered in the next lesson, but give students the chance to come up with some ideas now.)

7. Once students have started to consider these issues, distribute copies of "Geraldo's Reading Plan" worksheet and read it with students. Ask them to make a detailed plan for Geraldo. (The students might work in groups to develop this plan.) *Note:* While students will have to consider all of Geraldo's homework to make a good plan, their emphasis should be on strategies to help him with his reading difficulties.

Geraldo's Reading Plan

Directions

READ "Geraldo's Reading: A Case Study."
   FILL OUT THIS FORM to make a plan for Geraldo to get his science reading done.

1. Geraldo's *reading assignment*:

2. The *purpose* of Geraldo's reading assignment:

    (Examples: to answer questions, to prepare for a test, to prepare for discussion tomorrow)

3. *Reading strategies* that will help Geraldo to do this kind of reading:

    (Examples: reading slowly and carefully, skimming, note-taking, re-reading, making up questions about the reading, reading the questions before reading the book)

4. Geraldo's past *personal experience* with this kind of reading:

    (Is it easy or hard for him? Does it go quickly or slowly? Does it require a lot of concentration? When is he usually in the best frame of mind to tackle it? Where does he work best?)

5. *Other things* Geraldo needs to do tonight:

6. Make a specific *time plan* for Geraldo that will help him get the reading done:

    (Tell the specific order in which he should do his homework, the amount of time he should spend on each part of the homework, when he should start his homework, when he should take breaks.)

8. Once students have developed their plans, ask a few to share plans with the class. Point out the differences in the plans and explain that there can be many good ways to accomplish the same task: The important thing is for students to find the way that is best for *them*.

9. Now give students the opportunity to plan with their own needs in mind. Assign reading that you would normally give in the course of your curriculum. Distribute

copies of the "Personal Reading Plan" worksheet. Ask students to make a reading plan that will help them to get the reading done tonight. To fill in question 5, they might have to anticipate other homework they'll have. Tell them not to worry about questions 7 and 8 right now, and remind them that you will collect their plans along with their homework tomorrow.

10. Before collecting their plans the next day, have them write a short evaluation of how well the plan worked and what they might do differently the next time they make one. (You may want to use the "Evaluation of Personal Reading Plan" worksheet located in the Student Handout section at the end of this chapter.)

Connections

Homework Lesson 4.2: Knowing Your Personal Needs

Writing Lesson 3.2: Using Past Experiences in Writing

Writing Lesson 3.3: Getting Down to Work

Follow-Up Activity

Each time you give a reading assignment, ask students to make a plan for it. As the students get more familiar with their particular patterns and preferences, these plans (and the evaluations of them) could become more informal—perhaps a simple list or a brief reflection in their journals.

LESSON 2.4 Strategies for Thoughtful Reading

Central Themes

Knowing Process

Knowing Differences

Synopsis

Exercises and a discussion to help students develop strategies for reading various kinds of assignments efficiently and effectively.

What To Do

1. Make copies of the following handouts:

    - a list of six or seven typical school reading assignments (can be based on the list that students brainstormed in Lesson 1)
    - the "Personal Reading Plan" worksheet (included in the Student Handout section at the end of this chapter)
    - the "Evaluation of Personal Reading Plan" worksheet (included in the Student Handout section)

    You will also need a list of various reading strategies. This list should be put on the board. Either you can make it up ahead of time, or you can develop the list with the students in class.

2. Remind the students that different readings require different tactics. Give each student a copy of the list of reading assignments. The list should include such items as:

    - reading a short story that will be discussed in class tomorrow
    - reading a social studies chapter in order to answer questions at the end of it
    - reading a book in order to do a book report
    - reading a science chapter to get ready for a test
    - reading word problems in math
    - reading directions on a test or worksheet

3. Tell students that they're going to be considering different strategies for approaching these assignments.

4. Depending on how skilled your students are with different reading techniques, either have them brainstorm different techniques that they use when reading (write these techniques on the board as you go), or write an initial list on the board and let students add to it. Some possible strategies include:

- reading slowly and carefully to pick up details
- skimming for main ideas
- skimming titles, subheadings, graphs, maps, pictures, and captions, and then reading more carefully
- skimming to look for summaries embedded in the text, and carefully reading only the summaries
- reading the questions at the end first, and then reading to look for answers
- re-reading the material a second (or third) time
- taking notes (using key words, outlining, diagramming) while reading
- taking notes (using key words, diagramming) after reading
- some combination of the above

5. Start with the first assignment listed on their handouts and ask students what reading strategies they might use for this assignment and why. What strategies might be inappropriate and why? Students might write down their ideas first and then discuss them as a class.

6. Once students have gone through the list of assignments, give one of the reading assignments on the list (making it relevant to current class material). Ask students to fill out a "Personal Reading Plan" sheet and to use the strategies that they agreed would be useful for this type of assignment.

7. In class the next day, begin by asking students to fill out an "Evaluation of the Personal Reading Plan" worksheet. Alternately, have the students evaluate their plans in discussion. Ask several students to share the strategies they used and to say how well they worked. For strategies that didn't work, ask members of the class to help by suggesting other strategies that the student might use next time.

Connections

Homework Lesson 4.2: Knowing Your Personal Needs

Writing Lesson 3.3: Getting Down to Work

Testing Lesson 5.4: The Process of Taking Notes

Follow-Up Activity

For major reading assignments, ask students to do both a reading plan and a self-evaluation. On the day the assignment is due, hold a brainstorming and problem-solving session with your students around reading issues. Ask them to share any problems they were unable to solve, and ask the rest of the class to brainstorm possible solutions. Encourage students to enter particularly useful suggestions in their journals.

LESSON 2.5 Troubleshooting While Reading

Central Theme

Knowing Process

Synopsis

A survey and discussion to help students acquire strategies for addressing particular problems they encounter as they read.

What To Do

1. Prepare copies of the "Survey of Problems with Reading" (in the Student Handout section at the end of this chapter).

2. This sheet lists difficulties that students might encounter while reading. Ask students to rate the problems on a scale of 1 to 4: "1" means that they hardly ever encounter it; "4" means that they run into this problem almost all the time. Have the students work through the survey with you. Explain each item to the students and then have them answer it before you begin to explain the next item. Items 4 and 5 might be especially hard for students. You could use the example of a difficult short story for item 4. For item 5, tell them this would be like reading about a certain historical event in social studies, but not understanding why that event is important, or enjoying a short story, but not understanding its point.

Survey of Problems with Reading

Directions

Rate each one of the problems on a scale of 1 to 4.

  1 = I *almost never* have this difficulty.

  2 = I *sometimes* have this difficulty.

  3 = I experience this difficulty *a lot* of the time.

  4 = I have this difficulty *almost always*.

1. Not knowing the purpose of the reading (what your teacher wants you to get out of it)

          1   2   3   4

2. Getting distracted, bored, or tired while reading

       1   2   3   4

3. Not understanding words

       1   2   3   4

4. Understanding the words, but not being able to figure out what's happening

       1   2   3   4

5. Understanding what's happening, but not what is important or why

       1   2   3   4

6. Not being able to understand how the reading is important to me personally

       1   2   3   4

7. Other difficulties:

3. Ask students if they'd like to add any other difficulties to the list. Have them rate these as well.

4. Now work with your students to come up with specific strategies for addressing each of these problems. You might want to let their ratings guide you in how much emphasis you put on any one of these strategies. If many students give the problem a "four," take it seriously. However, don't ignore those items which many students rank as "one"—they simply might not yet recognize that problem in their reading. Below is a partial list of solutions that you can suggest if your students don't.

Some Solutions to the Survey Problems

1. Not knowing the purpose of the assignment

- Ask the teacher.
- Ask another student.

2. Getting distracted, tired, or bored by the reading

- Figure out how long you can concentrate at a time, and change your Reading Plan so that you take a break and do something else every so often (take a stretch or snack break, work on other homework).

- Write (notes, questions, diagrams, anything) while you read, to keep yourself alert.
- Imagine that you are the writer and, at the end of each paragraph or section, try to guess what you would write next. Read to see if your guess is correct.
- Try to relate something you know and enjoy to the reading topic.
- Imagine what the people or things in the reading look like; make a mental movie of what you're reading, or try to sketch the people and things in the text as you read.

3. Not understanding particular words

- Use a dictionary.
- Use context clues. Look for relevant information in the passage or for other instances of the word, fit the clues together in a way that makes sense, think about what you already know. (Worksheets in the Student Handout section address these skills.)
- Ask a friend, sibling, parent, or other person.
- Skip the word and see if things still make sense. (It might not be important.)

4. Understanding the words, but not being able to figure out what's happening

- Re-read, using a list or flow chart to keep track of events; when you don't understand what's happening, insert a question mark, leave a space, and keep listing.
- Keep reading. Maybe you'll come to a part that makes more sense.
- Try putting things in your own words.
- Ask a friend.
- Think of other things you have read that are like what you are reading now. What happened in those other readings? Could the same sort of thing be going on here?

5. Understanding what's happening, but not what is important or why

- After reading it once, skim to pick out only main ideas.
- Imagine you are the author: What point would you be trying to make?
- Ask yourself what the teacher might test you on.
- If you were making a comic strip, what things would you need to show?
- Examine chapter titles and subtitle headings: What clues do they provide?
- Talk with a friend.

6. Not understanding how the material is important to you personally

- If you are reading about a character or person whose life is very different from yours, try to think of things you might know about that person's life from watching television or movies or from reading other books. Picture yourself or a friend in that person's place.
- If you are reading about a place unfamiliar to you, travel there in your imagination. Pretend that you are walking there, or driving through it, or looking at it from a plane. Draw a picture of the place and, as you read, add new details.
- Make a list of the ways in which a person or place or event in the reading is similar to, as well as different from, you or a friend or a place you know well.

5. You might add your students' suggestions to this chart and distribute it so that students can use it to problem-solve while they read. Stress to them that, if they can't solve a problem, they should write out the most specific question they can and bring it to class.

Connections

Homework Lesson 4.3: Personal Solutions to Homework Difficulties

Homework Lesson 4.5: Resources

Testing Lesson 5.6: Understanding Test Questions

Follow-Up Activity

Post publically the problem-solving ideas students have generated for the problems many identified as particularly throublesome. Ask students to add to the list whenever they think of new ideas. Have them record in their journals the strategies that work best for them.

LESSON 2.6 Re-Reading

Central Theme

Re-reading

Synopsis

A discussion and some activities to help students see the importance of re-reading and to help them use this technique more effectively.

What To Do

1. Ask students about activities that they typically do more than once, like practicing a sport, watching a good movie, or listening to a favorite song. For each example they give, ask why they do it repeatedly. Keep track of their reasons on the board.

2. Ask students if they've ever read something more than once. If some say yes, ask why and make another list of their reasons on the board. If some say no, record their reasons.

3. Now compare the two lists: How is re-reading like re-doing other things? How is it different? In this discussion, it will be important to tackle directly two common objections to re-reading: "I don't need to re-read" and "Re-reading is boring."

4. For those who claim not to need it, acknowledge that sometimes they might *not* need to. Ask them to list a few things they feel they don't need to re-read and why they don't need to re-read them. Then ask them to think back to Lesson 1 of the section (or to look back in their journals) to see what kinds of reading they have found most problematic. Without forcing the issue, suggest that they might think about how re-reading could help them get the hard reading done well enough so that when test time comes they're better prepared.

5. For those who claim that re-reading is boring, acknowledge that it can be. If they haven't done so already, ask them to list some other problems with re-reading (it takes a lot of time, it doesn't really do any good). Then ask students to point out the advantages (which they may have already listed on the board): They can learn more; they can get better at reading; they can be prepared ahead of time for the test, instead of waiting to cram at the last minute; and so on. Admit that some important things aren't always fun, but that there are some ways of making re-reading more productive and, perhaps, a little more interesting.

6. Ask students if they can think of any tricks or techniques that would help them to re-read better. Keep track of their ideas. Add to the list any of the following ideas if they haven't suggested them already:

- *Hunting for the Unknown.* Look for three pieces of information that you don't remember seeing the first time you read. Write them down and decide whether or not they're important. If they are *all* important, try re-reading again to see if there are any other important things you missed.
- *Cross-Examine the Witness.* Pretend that the reading assignment is like a witness in the courtroom, telling you about something that happened. After you've read it once ("heard the testimony"), think about what points or ideas you want the witness to clarify. Write down three questions, and then re-read ("cross-examine") the witness, trying to find answers to your questions. (If you don't find the answers, make sure to ask your teacher about them the next day.)
- *Read and Write.* Give yourself a break and don't take any notes at all the first time you read something. Just read straight through. If you get stuck, don't worry too much about it. Skip the hard parts and go on to where the reading gets easier. Then, when you re-read, get your paper and pencil out. Use note-taking skills from Lessons 3 and 4 in the Testing section. Or use some of the mapping strategies described in Lesson 4 of this section.
- *Be Your Teacher.* When you re-read, pretend that you are your teacher and that you are planning a test on this reading. Make up test questions that you would ask to make sure your students *really* understood the material. Think up report topics and discussion questions as well.

7. Before ending this discussion, remind students that whether they re-read depends on the *kind* and *purpose* of the reading they have to do, as well as on their *personal needs* and how much *time* they have. Point out that learning to make decisions about when and how to re-read is not an easy task, but one that will become easier with practice.

8. Assign a reading selection for homework—something that your students would probably need to read twice. Ask your students to discuss whether re-reading this assignment would be useful and why. Then ask them to pick one of the strategies and use it to re-read the assignment. In class the next day, ask the students to write in their self-profile journals a short evaluation of the technique: Did it help or not? Why or why not?

Connections

Writing Lesson 3.5: What's the Point of Revising?

Writing Lesson 3.6: A Revision Process

Follow-Up Activity

For the next few weeks, when you assign reading ask students to pick and use a different technique until they've had a chance to try them all. Ask them to note in their journals the ones that work particularly well as well as the ones that don't work at all. Encourage them to refer to their journals to review these tips before they begin particularly difficult reading assignments.

Student Handouts

For *Lesson 3: Personal Reading Profiles and Plans*
- "Geraldo's Reading: A Practice Case"
- "Geraldo's Reading Plan" Worksheet
- "Personal Reading Plan" Worksheet
- "Evaluation of Personal Reading Plan" Worksheet

For *Lesson 5: Troubleshooting While Reading*
- "Survey of Problems with Reading"

Geraldo's Reading: A Practice Case

Directions

READ the information on this page about Geraldo's homework and his reading profile.

DECIDE the best way for Geraldo to do his science reading, as well as the rest of his homework.

Geraldo's Homework

- Read Chapter 7 (five pages long) in his science book and answer the ten questions at the end of the chapter

- Solve 20 math problems

- Do a short worksheet on verbs for language arts

Geraldo's Reading Profile

- He *hates* science reading because
  1. it is hard to understand;
  2. it takes him a long time to complete.

- He likes math homework the best because it doesn't involve any reading.

- When he tries to read, the television set often distracts him—but his favorite show comes on right after school.

- He can't really concentrate on difficult reading for more than 15 minutes at a time.

- He's usually tired and in a bad mood when he gets home from school.

Geraldo's Reading Plan

Directions

READ "Geraldo's Reading: A Case Study."

FILL OUT THIS FORM to make a plan for Geraldo to get his science reading done.

1.   Geraldo's *reading assignment*:

2.   The *purpose* of Geraldo's reading assignment:
     (Examples: to answer questions, to prepare for a test, to prepare for discussion tomorrow)

3.   *Reading strategies* that will help Geraldo to do this kind of reading:
     (Examples: reading slowly and carefully, skimming, note-taking, rereading, making up questions about the reading, reading the questions before reading the passage)

4.   Geraldo's past *personal experience* with this kind of reading:

>   (Is it easy or hard for him? Does it go quickly or slowly? Does it require a lot of concentration? When is he usually in the best frame of mind to tackle it? Where does he work best?)

5.   *Other things* Geraldo needs to do tonight:

6.   Make a specific *time plan* for Geraldo that will help him get the reading done:

>   (Tell the specific order in which he should do his homework, the amount of time he should spend on each part of the homework, when he should start his homework, when he should take breaks.)

Personal Reading Plan

1.   Your *reading assignment*:

2.   The *purpose* of the reading assignment:
     (to answer questions, to prepare for a test, to prepare for discussion to-morrow)

3.   *Reading strategies* that will help you to do this assignment:
     (Examples: reading slowly and carefully, skimming, note-taking, re-reading, making up questions about the reading, reading the questions before reading the passage)

4.   Your past *personal experience* with this kind of reading:
     (Is it easy or hard for you? Does it go quickly or slowly? Does it re-quires a lot of concentration? When are you usually in the best frame of mind to tackle it? Where do you work best?)

5.   *Other things* you need to do tonight:

6.   Make a specific *time plan* that will help you get the reading done:
     (Tell the specific order in which you should do your homework, the amount of time you should spend on each part of the homework, when you should start the homework, when you should take breaks.)

7.   Is re-reading a good idea for this assignment? Why or why not?

8.   Re-reading strategy or strategies that you used:

Evaluation of Personal Reading Plan

(to be done the day after the reading assignment has been completed)

1. Did you stick to your plan?

2. If yes, do you think it helped you?

3. If no, why not?

4.   Did you allot the right amount of time for doing all your work well? What took longer than you expected? What was shorter?

5.   What problems did you encounter as you read?

6.   How did you solve these problems?

7.   What should you do differently the next time you have this kind of assignment?

Survey of Problems with Reading

Directions

Rate each one of the problems on a scale of 1 to 4.

1 = I *almost never* have this difficulty.

2 = I *sometimes* have this difficulty.

3 = I experience this difficulty *a lot* of the time.

4 = I have this difficulty *almost always*.

1. Not knowing the purpose of the reading (what my teacher wants me to get out of it)

    1   2   3   4

2. Getting distracted, bored, or tired while reading

    1   2   3   4

3. Not understanding words

    1   2   3   4

4. Understanding the words, but not being able to figure out what's happening

    1   2   3   4

5. Understanding what's happening, but not what is important or why

    1   2   3   4

6. Not being able to understand how the reading is important to me personally

    1   2   3   4

7. Other difficulties:

CHAPTER 3

Expository Writing

Wendy M. Williams and Robert J. Sternberg

Contents

Expository Writing Themes

1. Knowing Why
   - Understanding the importance of writing in and out of school.
   - Understanding differences between written information and other types of information.
2. Knowing Self
   - Recognizing current writing practices.
   - Identifying personal strengths and weaknesses in terms of writing.
   - Knowing how to incorporate one's interests and expertise into writing assignments.
3. Knowing Differences
   - Knowing how to write for different types of assignments and audiences.
   - Knowing different styles of, and strategies for, writing.
4. Knowing Process
   - Understanding how writing involves planning and organization.
   - Knowing strategies and resources to overcome difficulties in writing.
5. Reworking
   - Understanding the importance of revision.
   - Knowing how to revise.

About the Writing Chapter

Writing instruction is a part of every academic curriculum, but there's also much to teach students about the practical side of writing. This section of the PIFS curriculum covers the five PIFS themes as they apply to expository writing.

The lessons discuss why writing is important in and out of school, and how the written word is special. Students will uncover their strengths and weaknesses in writing and learn how to incorporate their strengths into writing assignments. The lessons also explore writing for different types of assignments and audiences, and recommend strategies to make writing effective.

The writing process itself is the subject of lessons that help students appreciate the role of planning and organization in good writing. The all-too-common problem of writer's block is discussed here, along with strategies for overcoming problems while writing. Finally, the topic of revision is addressed in lessons that stress both the importance of revising and knowing how best to go about it.

The PIFS writing curriculum is designed as a supplement to a standard writing curriculum. In it you will find new approaches to old problems, useful worksheets, and other teaching aids to help your students tackle the practical side of writing. The PIFS approach will help students develop not only an understanding of why they should learn to write but also solid writing skills that will last into adulthood.

The Five Themes

Lesson 1 emphasizes "knowing why."

Lesson 2 emphasizes "knowing self" and "knowing process."

Lesson 3 emphasizes "knowing self" and "knowing process."

Lesson 4 emphasizes "knowing self" and "knowing process."

Lesson 5 emphasizes "knowing why" and "reworking."

Lesson 6 emphasizes "knowing differences," "knowing process," and "reworking."

Lesson 7 emphasizes "knowing differences" and "knowing process."

Lesson 8 emphasizes "knowing differences" and "knowing process."

Overview of the Lessons

The place and purpose of writing (and reading) in their lives is easy for students to overlook, given all the video images and music and socializing that fill many students' after-school time. Nevertheless, writing, like reading, *does* have a place (however small for now) outside of school for these students. **Lesson 1**, in reminding students of this point and helping them to think about the role of writing in their future, can help to put a seemingly pointless school task into perspective.

Examining past experiences with writing can be an important first step toward improving future writing. **Lesson 2** helps students draw upon past experiences (both in school and out) with domains other than writing that can hook students into projects they would otherwise find unengaging. By encouraging students to incorporate other strengths into their writing, this lesson ensures that even those students who are not particularly gifted linguistically will have an opportunity to enjoy and succeed in writing. The lesson also helps students use information across subject areas in more creative and practical ways.

Completing projects assigned by someone else is an integral part of daily life both in school and, for many of us, later in life. However, learning to shape an

assignment to personal interests within certain imposed constraints takes practice. Students can also be trapped by force of habit into one mode of writing
(usually "report" style) without recognizing that different writing assignments
call for different approaches.

Lesson 3 asks students to consider several alternative formats before beginning a project to encourage deeper, more imaginative thinking and to decrease
the possibility that they will choose an approach simply because it was the first
idea that occurred to them. This lesson also demonstrates that considering alternative writing approaches helps students to pick formats and styles of writing appropriate to the task and subject matter at hand.

A host of problems can assail students as they pass the planning stage and
attempt the first draft. Deadlines, unexpected lack of resources, and a dearth of
ideas can all lead to frustration, which, in turn, limits productivity, despite students' best efforts. In Lesson 4, students discuss these problems and brainstorm
solutions that can better prepare them for dealing with troubles during the
writing process.

Perhaps no part of the writing process is as difficult to master as revision.
Lesson 5 and Lesson 6 both address this topic, with the emphasis of Lesson 5
being "the point of revising" and that of Lesson 6 being the revision process itself. Many students do not understand why revision is important. Students often are unwilling to make the effort to revise their own work; they view writing
as a single-step activity akin to taking a test. Whatever they write down the first
time is their "answer," and it's up to the teacher to decide whether that answer
is right or wrong. When asked to rewrite, students conclude that the first draft
must have been wrong—even a waste of time. Couple this verdict with the fact
that writing the *first* draft is often laborious and time-consuming work, and it's
little wonder that students resist revising. Who likes to dwell on her own mistakes? Who likes to recognize that mistakes seem to crop up in spite of his best
efforts?

The students who can be coached across the first hurdle of accepting that revision is often necessary are immediately confronted by a second hurdle: the
problem of procedure, the focus of Lesson 6. Some think that making any
change for any reason (and sometimes for no reason in particular) constitutes a
valid revision. Many students do not know what they should be trying to
change about their papers. Organization? Ideas? Word choice? They are willing
to try to make their writing better, but what does "better" mean? Better for
whom? Better for what?

The first part of Lesson 6 is designed to help students enter quickly and easily into the revision process by reducing their self-investment in the first draft.
The second and third parts help to broaden the students' conception of revision
by shifting the emphasis from correcting mistakes to providing detail and tai-

loring the work for a specific audience. Ultimately, students should learn that revision is best carried out with a specific goal in mind, and specific ideas about how to reach that goal.

When assigned a written report, students often copy text from its sources. By doing so, they defeat the purposes of writing reports, such as learning new information, demonstrating an ability to use and synthesize a variety of resource materials, showing comprehension through reporting the material in their own words, and demonstrating an ability to organize information. To avoid the pitfalls of copying, and to encourage a true understanding of new information, **Lesson 7** introduces students to the variety of formats available when they are assigned written reports. These formats are designed to encourage creative, original thought.

Lesson 8 promotes students' awareness of the many and varying resources that exist as potential sources of information. Recognizing what constitutes information, knowing where information can be found, and understanding the limitations of various types of information are essential to success in virtually every endeavor. Usually, the most interesting types and sources of information are not the traditional sources students think about. Often, they never look beyond dictionaries and encyclopedias to the many alternative sources available to them, such as newspapers, personal interviews with community members, trips to local museums, and so on. This lesson underscores the fact that success in school and in life is often not so much a matter of *knowing* the right answer as being able to *find it out*.

Suggested Teaching Sequence

The sequence of lessons is not fixed. Infusion of the lessons into existing curriculum is encouraged, as is the revisiting of lessons. Teachers should feel free to revise as necessary.

Acknowledgements

Portions of Lessons 5, 6, 7, and 8 were drafted by Toby Caplin, a fifth/sixth-grade teacher in Cambridge, Massachusetts, based on ideas developed in her practice. Melanie Gordon Brigockas, a researcher at Yale University, contributed to the follow-up activities.

LESSON 3.1 Writing In School and Out

Central Theme

Knowing Why

Synopsis

A brainstorm and a discussion to help students see the various uses of writing both in and out of school, both now and in the future.

What To Do

1. Brainstorm with students all the times in the past weeks when they've written something out of school (writing tasks such as taking telephone messages and writing notes to friends *count*).

2. Then have them list all the writing they've done in school: essays, answering questions at the back of textbooks, notes, journal entries.

3. Ask them to conjecture about the various kinds of writing that might be used in adult careers. Students can break up into groups to see who can come up with the most ways that adults use writing in occupations. (They could write letters to various celebrities or to adults in the community and ask what parts of their jobs involve writing. In addition to enabling students to collect "real world" information about writing, this activity offers the benefit of allowing students to write for a real audience. Display responses on a bulletin board.)

4. Compare the lists.
   - How is school writing like the writing they do outside of school or the writing that adults do for their jobs?
   - How is it different?
   - With videos, tape recorders, and telephones, why does anyone bother to write?
   - What would your life be like if you couldn't write?
   - What sorts of information would be lost if there were no such thing as writing?

5. If students do write letters, keep these lists of writing activities handy. When the replies come in, let students check to see if their conjectures were right, or add to the lists.

Connections

Testing Lesson 5.3: The Importance of Taking Notes

Reading Lesson 2.1: Why Read?

Follow-Up Activity

Ask students to compare the lists they drew up in this lesson to those they developed in the "why read" discussion (Thoughtful Reading, Lesson 1). How similar are the two lists? Does the comparison suggest new items that should be added to one list or the other? How interrelated are the skills of reading and writing? Can someone be a good reader and have trouble with writing? And vice versa? Do the students think they are better readers than writers (or vice versa)? If they feel that they are better at one than the other, are there techniques that they use when doing one that might help them with the other?

LESSON 3.2 Using Past Experiences in Writing

Central Themes

Knowing Self

Knowing Process

Synopsis

Journal writing, discussion, and brainstorms to help students reflect both on their past experiences with writing and on the extracurricular interests and strengths that might help them in their writing.

What To Do

1. Provide students with a copy of the list of different types of writing that they brainstormed on the first day (Writing, Lesson 1). Have them refer to it when answering the following questions (in their journals) about their past experiences with writing:

    *   What kind of writing do you like doing the most?
    *   What is the easiest or most enjoyable thing about doing that kind of writing?
    *   What kind of writing do you like the least?
    *   What is the hardest or least enjoyable thing about doing that kind of writing?
    *   When and where do you do your best writing?
    *   What circumstances make it hard for you to write?
    *   What do you like to write about?
    *   Do you prefer the writing assignments of one subject to those of other subjects?
    *   Is there a specific kind of assignment that you enjoy doing no matter what class it's for?

2. Spend a few minutes talking with students about the things they find easiest and hardest about writing. Are there trends across the class? Students will probably find that the writing they do outside of school is almost always easier and more enjoyable than the writing they do in school. This is understandable, given that the writing they do outside of class is usually voluntary and done to accomplish purposes that they see as relevant to their lives. Not having chosen their school assignments, and perhaps not understanding their importance in either the long or short run, students find them more work and much less fun.

3. Ask students to look through the first pages of their self-profile journals, where they listed all their strengths and interests when they were doing activities from the Introduction lessons. Explain that they can use these interests to help them become

more interested in, and so improve at, writing assignments. They can incorporate their interests, experiences, and strengths into their assignments.

4. Give the class a report topic that comes from the normal curriculum for this week (something that you would have assigned anyway). The best topics for this exercise are fairly focused, but not so much as to prevent the students from shaping the topics to their thoughts. Write the report topic on the board. For the purposes of illustration, let's say that your class is currently studying colonial America.

5. Have each student think of at least three ideas for a writing assignment (e.g., a writing project or report) about this topic that could incorporate a personal interest or area of expertise. (You might want to do a few out loud to help students get the hang of it.) Lists might include ideas like these:

    - *Drawing.* Focus on a topic that lends itself to illustrations (types of dress or housing).
    - *Computer/video games.* Design and write a manual for a role-playing game about life in colonial times; players might win or lose points depending on how well they survive the boat trip, make friends with natives, build weather-resistant homes, and so on.
    - *Acting.* Write a play about some aspect of life in colonial America.
    - *Skateboarding.* Report on transportation in colonial times (how people got around, how much people traveled, who traveled).
    - *Making up stories.* Write some diary entries of a colonial teenager.
    - *Medicine.* Write about illnesses and cures common in colonial America.
    - *Food.* Write a few entries for a colonial cookbook; recipes could include ingredients available to colonial Americans, tips for how to store food, cooking devices.
    - *Getting into trouble with the law.* Describe what people in colonial America could be punished for, as well as how they were punished.
    - *Entertainment.* Write about what young people did for fun in colonial America.
    - *Music.* Describe the music people liked then, and how people listened to it. (If the writing requirements are loose, students might also write a rap or song about an event like the Boston Tea Party or the Salem witch trials.)
    - *Animals.* What animals did people in colonial America use for pets? What animals did they hunt, or did they fear? How were animals a part of their daily lives?

6. Ask some of the students to share their ideas from this exercise. For each idea, have the class brainstorm a few possible sources of information (*besides* a textbook or encyclopedia) that might be helpful to consult.

7. Ask if anyone had an interest that he or she just couldn't relate to the topic in any way. If so, see if the class as a group has any ideas. Consider: Are there certain things that simply won't relate to the given topic? Are there ways of looking at an interest in a broader light that might make it relate better to the topic (as in the earlier skateboarding example)?

8. Discuss the advantages and disadvantages of choosing these more unusual topics. Conclude by stressing that every assignment has a certain amount of leeway in

how it may be approached. It's up to the student to work a personal interest into the topic to enliven the assignment for both the writer *and* the reader.

Connections

Writing Lesson 3.7: Choosing a Format

Reading Lesson 2.3: Personal Reading Profiles

Homework Lesson 4.6: Making It More Interesting and Personal

Follow-Up Activity

Have the students log in their journals for each writing assignment how they have incorporated their interests or how they have otherwise helped themselves relate to the topic.

LESSON 3.3 Getting Down To Work

Central Themes

Knowing Self

Knowing Process

Synopsis

A planning activity in which students begin a writing assignment by brainstorming and then thinking through three possible ways of carrying it out. With the use of a planning sheet, students consider the teacher's requirements, their own interests, the available resources, and the time constraints.

What To Do

1. Prepare copies of the following handouts (included in the Student Handout section):
   - "Planning Sheet for Writing Assignments"
   - "Susanna's Writing Plan"

2. Explain to students that writing assignments, like other kinds of homework or projects, require some planning and organizing.

3. Distribute the two handouts. Let students know that the planning sheet is a tool for planning their work and organizing both their ideas and their time. You can introduce how to use the sheet by reading aloud "Susanna's Writing Plan" and then having the class as a group fill out a planning sheet for her. Use the information in steps 5 and 6 below to guide you.

Susanna's Writing Plan

Directions

Use the information provided about Susanna to design a plan to help her get her writing assignment done well and on time.

Susanna's Assignment

Write a two-page report on some aspect of life or writing of the author Mark Twain. The report is due in one week.

Susanna's Writing Profile

Susanna doesn't mind writing but
  1. never knows how to begin her papers.
  2. is not sure where to make her paragraphs.
Susanna's personal interests are traveling, dancing, and animals.

Susanna likes to do her writing at home in her room.

Susanna likes to give her own opinions in her writing.

Susanna has read *Tom Sawyer*, a book by Mark Twain.

Susanna likes speaking in front of the classroom and making other people laugh.

Make a writing plan for Susanna using the writing plan handout.

4. After practicing with the Susanna scenario, give students their own writing assignment. The planning sheets work best when the assigned writing project is one in which you suggest a general topic and allow students to make choices about their own specific focus, approach, and format. If the writing assignment is a relatively simple one, you can ask students to cross out the spaces for "resources" and "possible modes of presentation."

5. Talk the students through the first part of the sheet, helping them to fill in the "teacher requirements" at the top of the page: the general topic, the required length, the due date, and any other restrictions or guidelines.

PLANNING SHEET

Teacher Requirements: Subject: Kind of project: Length: Due date: Other guidelines:			
Ideas & Possibilities:	1	2	3
Possible topics			
Connections with personal interests previous projects			
Possible resources			
Possible modes of presentation			

Feedback notes

6. Explain to the students that, in order to fill out the rest of the blocks on the sheet, they need to imagine three different ways they can meet your requirements—three different ways they can go about writing the paper.

    - What are their personal interests that connect with the general topic?
    - What might their interests, experiences, or previous writing projects suggest about which aspects of the given topic they should concentrate on?
    - What resources will each possibility require?
    - What are some possible ways of organizing and presenting the material?

Ask students to generate more than one possibility within each block on the sheet. Once they have completed their planning sheets, they can then choose whichever of their two or three plans seems most promising. (See the **"Notes"** section following for more information on formats and resources.)

If students think that this is a lot of unnecessary work, talk with them about times in their lives when they've had to carry out some project and how a little serious thinking before they began might have saved them some trouble in the long run.

    - Have they ever started to bake cookies and then discovered that they didn't have all the ingredients?
    - Have they tried to coordinate a trip to the movies with some friends—and it took a hundred phone calls back and forth between five people before they finally figured out which movie (and which showing) to go to, when to get together, and where to meet?
    - Have they had ideas for building a bike ramp, or sewing a dress, or writing a song—and the more they thought about it, the better their ideas got?

Ask students to consider if the projects would have been as good if they had started to carry out the first idea that came to them. Writing works the same way.

7. If time permits, allow the students to gather in small groups to discuss their chosen plans of action. Each member of the group reads her chosen plan to the other members. The members respond by suggesting other resources the student may not have considered, offering other possible ways to present the material, and perhaps pointing out other related aspects of the student's topic that they themselves find interesting and would like to know about.

8. Have students carry out the writing assignments they have planned. When they hand in their papers, ask them to write a brief evaluation of how the planning sheet helped or didn't help them with their writing.

Notes

You may find it helpful to give a writing assignment prior to Lesson 3 that will be comparable to the one described in Lesson 3. That way students will have two writing assignments—one with the planning sheet, one without. When both assignments have been completed, the class can discuss how their strategies, approaches, and results differed with and without planning.

Formats. Lesson 7, Choosing a Format. provides some alternative ways of carrying out writing assignments. If you don't have time to do this lesson with your class, you might simply suggest some of these formats to them when the writing assignments seem to lend themselves to such alternatives.

Resources. Students will be more adept at coming up with various resources (newspapers, interviews, site visits, city bureaus, information hot-lines, classmates, school personnel) if they have had some previous preparation in using alternatives to the standard encyclopedia. *Lesson 8, Using a Variety of Resources,* considers this issue more fully. For now, suggest alternatives to the students and encourage them to brainstorm their own resource suggestions.

Connections

Writing Lessons 3.7 & 3.8: See Formats and Resources sections above

Introduction Lesson 1.3: Sharing Talents

Introduction Lesson 1.5: Individual Differences in School

Reading Lesson 2.3: Personal Reading Profiles

Reading Lesson 2.4: Strategies for Thoughtful Reading

Homework Lesson 4.2: Knowing Your Personal Needs

Homework Lesson 4.5: Getting Organized

Follow-Up Activity

Have students record in their journals their own writing profile using the one for Susanna as a guide. Ask them to amend it for each new writing project, as their habits or experiences change, and as each new writing task makes new demands on them. This profile will be more succinct and project-oriented than the one they wrote during Lesson 2 of this section.

LESSON 3.4 Getting Unstuck

Central Themes

Knowing Self

Knowing Process

Synopsis

An activity designed to show students how to cope with problems they encounter in the process of completing a first draft.

What To Do

1. Prepare copies of the following handouts (from the Student Handout section):

    • "Writer's Block and Other Problems Worksheet"
    • "Writer's Block Scenarios"

2. Ask students to look back at the list of writing difficulties they recorded in their journals during Writing Lesson 2.

3. Distribute copies of the handout, "Writer's Block and Other Problems Worksheet." You might want to talk about the symptoms of writer's block for those students who may not recognize the label. Describe how it feels to be poised and ready for writing . . . and then to be overcome with sweaty palms, foreboding empty pages or computer screens, feelings of being ridiculed for not producing, knowledge that it's a beautiful day outside . . . and so on. Speak from your own experience about problems in actually committing words to paper. Bear in mind that students may not want to admit problems, but may still be having them. An alternative approach to this worksheet is to have students come up with the symptoms instead of using a top-down approach.

4. Now make the concept of writers block more concrete for students by using the "Writer's Block Scenarios" handout and asking the class to complete a planning sheet for each of the students in the handout.

Writer's Block Scenarios

Directions

Help the following students overcome writer's block by analyzing why they are having problems and suggesting what they can do to get unstuck.

Student 1: Ed

Ed is writing a one-page science paper about how the human heart works. It is due in two days. He just finished reading in his science book about the heart, but already he can't remember what it said. He looked *heart* up in the dictionary, but it didn't say very much. His parents aren't at home, and now he's just sitting in his room listening to music. What can he do?

Student 2: Tasha

Tasha has to write a five-line rhyming poem for language arts class. It is due tomorrow. The poem can be about anything Tasha wants. She wrote the first line, "My bike can go so fast," but then she got stuck, and she's been trying for ten minutes to think of what to do next. Now she feels really angry and doesn't want to work on the poem any more. What can she do?

Student 3: Chris

Chris has to write a summary of the major events of Abraham Lincoln's life. He has one week to write the summary. His teacher told him to look up the information at the library or at home, but he doesn't have a library card, and his family doesn't have that kind of book at home. Chris is really interested in Abraham Lincoln, but he figures he can't do this assignment because he can't get the information. What can he do?

5. After they've completed the worksheets, ask students to look for patterns in their own writing problems (they always get stuck during English reports but never during science reports, they never know how to start an assignment, and so on). Encourage students to explore the subjects in which the problems occur, as well as other factors (time of day, hunger level, state of relaxation, mood). It will also be helpful to have students review the Homework Questionnaire they completed in Lesson 2 of the Homework chapter.

6. Next, discuss students' tricks and strategies for overcoming their writing problems. Share some of your own strategies as well. Suggest that students fill in the strategy checklist at the bottom of the "Writing Problems" worksheet and keep it handy in their notebooks for consultation throughout the year. Begin the discussion with students' own ideas. In the course of the discussion, you might suggest some of the following strategies if students don't mention them.

Getting Motivated to Start Writing

- Give yourself five minutes during which you must scribble words, phrases, and sentences as fast as possible without regard to their neatness, grammar, and so forth. At the end of this time, re-read and circle the ideas that seem the most important. Try to organize these ideas into an outline, grouping together ideas that seem to belong together. If you need more ideas, pick a good one from the first five-minute free-writing and try to write for five more minutes about that. It's often a good start.
- Write an outline. Group together ideas that belong together, and put them in an order that you think makes sense. Sometimes the fill-in words come more easily after an outline exists, and an outline isn't that daunting.
- Tape yourself talking about the topic for a few minutes. Listen and transcribe what you said if it's good. If talking to yourself doesn't work, try talking to a classmate, your mom, your cat, or whomever.
- If you're hungry, tired, or tense, try to do something about it (eat, nap, take a walk) and then return to work.
- Visualize yourself finishing the assignment, handing it in, and receiving praise and a good grade. Think positively. Focus on the good feelings that come from completing a task.

Getting Organized During the Writing Process

- Consider what information your reader needs to know at the beginning of your essay or writing project so that the rest of it will make sense.
- Think about the priority of your ideas in the way you present your topic. The order in which you present information can affect the reader's understanding, build suspense, make your argument more convincing, and grab the reader's interest. Pay attention to the order of your ideas and paragraphs.
- The opening lines of an essay, and the beginning sentences of individual paragraphs within an essay, are very important in keeping the reader interested. Work on making these clear, topic-related, and attention-getting.

7. Give students a writing assignment. A slightly challenging one will be best. Ask them to pick two strategies to try if they get stuck while trying to complete it. In class the next day, ask them to write in their journals a brief evaluation of how those strategies worked for them.

Connections

Homework Lesson 4.2: Knowing Your Personal Needs

Homework Lesson 4.5: Resources

Testing Lesson 5.8: Troubleshooting During a Test

Follow-Up Activity

After students have completed several writing assignments and have recorded in their journals the strategies they used to help them, ask the students to review these strategies. Did they consistently use the same ones? Were different strategies appropriate for different papers? Were the strategies effective? Have students compare their success on the various writing assignments with the strategies used. From this, have them reevaluate how they might approach their next writing assignment.

LESSON 3.5 What's the Point of Revising?

Central Themes

Knowing Why

Reworking

Synopsis

Discussion, examples, and analogies to make revision less threatening, more motivating, and more purposeful for students.

What To Do

1. Prepare copies of the following handouts (from the Student Handout section at the end of this chapter):

    - "Paragraphs Needing Revision"
    - "Revising for Clarity: A Recipe"

2. No student will put his heart into revising unless it is emotionally safe for him to do so. The first step in learning how to revise is understanding that revision is a tool used by virtually every writer. *Everybody* does it. Discuss this with your students, using one or both of the following ideas to illustrate the point:

    - Even people who write for a living (the people who are *best* at it) often make messes of their first drafts. Bring in some of your own rough drafts, perhaps of worksheets or class handouts you've made up. Perhaps a local journalist or editor will share with the class a copy of a first draft of a story and a copy of the way it appeared in the newspaper.
    - Let the students work with you on revising writing, using the short sample paragraphs in the first handout or the recipe in the second. If you prefer, you may use something you yourself have written. If you use your own work, let the students know that you worked hard on it, and model how to receive criticisms and incorporate them into your work.

Paragraphs for Revision

Directions

Help these students revise their paragraphs to improve their writing. Check for spelling and grammatical errors. Do you think the sentences are in a good order? Can anything be left out? Is anything unclear? Should more information be added? What would you change, and why?

1. My house in the woods. There is a big yard, well kind of big, in front, and a hill in the back. We go there a lot in the different seasons of the year but mostly in the season of July. It is made of bricks and wood and has a bunch of rooms. It smells sometimes. The house is in New Hampshere. I think it has six rooms, not counting the bathroom.

2. I went to a concert and saw madona. It was awesome, there were maybe 20,000 people there. She sang alot of her songs, like "Papa Dont Preach and Cherish." She was realy great, and her dancers were realy great too. It was an awesome show. Wicked awesome!!!! Id go again.

3. My favorite subject is math because in math you get to use numbers and you don't have to read a whole lot and its pretty easy I think. Social studies is OK too but sometimes boring. Math is best I don't mind science but sometimes it is too hard because I don't understand all the words and so I can't understand what things mean. English is the worst it is too hard.

Revising for Clarity: A Recipe

Directions

If you have ever used a recipe or tried to assemble something using directions, you know that if the instructions are not clear, it's very confusing! This recipe needs revision. Decide where it is unclear, and rewrite it so that it makes more sense.

Scottish Shortbread Pan Cookies

Ingredients: 2 cups sifted flour

baking powder

salt

1 cup soft butter

½ confectioners sugar

Sift together flour, baking powder, and salt. Mix butter with sugar until very light and fluffy. Mix in flour. Refrigerate. Put chilled dough into pan. Bake 20–25 minutes. Cut while warm.

3.   After providing the students with some emotional reassurance about revision, offer them some examples of how revision is carried out in activities other than writing (activities in which revision seems natural, necessary, and nonthreatening). Try one or more of the following examples:

- *Revising as movie-making.* Filming a scene for a movie or television show often involves many "takes," just as writing a particular assignment often involves many drafts. Show the students (a section of) a how-they-made-the-movie video like "The Making of *Raiders of the Lost Ark*" or "A Day In The Life of *Family Ties*." These documentaries show directors, camerapersons, actors, and sometimes even writers discussing, revising, and re-shooting scenes in order to solve a wide variety of problems. A discussion following the film can help lead students to make connections between the re-takes in the movies and the revisions in their writing.

- *Revising as sports practice.* Revising in writing serves the same purpose as practicing in sports. A basketball player might set herself the goal of improving her outside jump shot. When the ball rims out, she knows she's done something wrong and has to think about how to change her form. Here, a coach or another player watching her can point out mistakes that she herself might not recognize. It might take hours of practice (and many revisions) before she can make the shot consistently. And even an NBA pro who can hit the jump shot with astounding proficiency will continue to try small alterations to make it faster or harder to defend against.

- *Revising as deciding what to wear.* This is a form of revision most students will recognize. In order to create a certain "look," they end up trying on many different combinations of clothes and accessories, each outfit representing a new revision. Students should know that just because they've taken off jeans and put on dress pants doesn't mean that jeans should *never* be worn—but that good pants are more appropriate for certain purposes, such as looking dressed up for class pictures. Similarly, in their writing, students may have to revise sections not because they are "wrong," but simply because they are inappropriate for the purpose of a particular assignment.

- *Revising as . . . ?* Ask students to think of other activities that involve the doing-evaluating-changing-redoing cycle. The activities can be things they do or things they know others do. The students can describe how they think these activities are similar (or not) to revision in writing.

Some important points to be made with the use of these analogies

- Revision is the opportunity to make sure that you are saying what you want to say in a way that others can understand. People may misunderstand you if you do not revise for clarity.

- People often revise with specific goals in mind. Rather than simply trying to make what they're doing "better," revisers aim to achieve specific effects: Steven Spielberg tries to make a scene more suspenseful; Michael Jordan tries to make his jump shot quicker; Judy Blume tries to make the situation in a particular chapter more realistic.
- Revising first drafts doesn't mean that they were wrong or a waste of time. Even if what you end up with doesn't look anything like what you started with, that first attempt was an essential part of the trial-and-error process.
- Getting feedback from others can be enormously helpful in coming up with an effective final draft.

Connections

Reading Lesson 2.6: Re-reading

Follow-Up Activity

Ask students to write in their journals about a time they rewrote something because they thought it needed to be done, not because someone made them do it. If they can't remember a time, have them write about a rewriting task a friend or relative undertook. What were the advantages and disadvantages? For students, there will always be disadvantages to a task that requires time and work. Try to bring out the positive emotional rewards of the task.

LESSON 3.6 A Revision Process

Central Themes

Knowing Differences

Knowing Process

Reworking

Synopsis

A writing activity designed to help students practice revising, and a recipe to keep their revising efforts focused.

What To Do

1. Have students write a first draft. You can use a writing assignment that you normally give at this time. Or you can try the following: Ask students to write a short paragraph that gives directions to someone their own age for doing a simple task (like throwing a ball or playing tic-tac-toe). You can allow students to choose their own topic as long as they select a procedure with a definite endpoint that can be described in a brief paragraph.

2. Limit the amount of time students spend on this first draft to ensure that they will not finish in one sitting. Warn the students in advance of the time constraint and assure them that they will have a chance to finish on the following day. (By limiting the amount of time students spend on the first draft, you also limit the amount of energy students invest in it. This will make it easier for them to revise their work when they return to the assignment.)

3. On the following day, remind students of what they discussed in the previous lesson: that revision is a directed process. When people revise they have specific goals in mind, and often they have specific ways of achieving these goals.

4. Return the first drafts to the students. At the top of their papers in the upper margin, ask them to write the following questions in a column: What? Who? How?

What? asks what they are hoping to accomplish in this paragraph. In the example case, the answer would be "giving directions for _____."

Who? asks for which specific audience the students are writing. For many assignments, the answer will be "my teacher." For this assignment, "my friends" or "someone my age" would be appropriate. Discuss also how the writer is also a part of his or her audience. (See **Notes** section following for more discussion about audience.)

How? is shorthand for "How am I going to make this paper better for the audience I am writing for?"

5.   The students will already know, or will quickly remember, the pertinent answers for the first two questions. This was information they were given when they began the assignment. The "How?" is the crucial question to be answered before they begin revising. With the students, brainstorm on the board all the things they could do to their papers to make them more appropriate for an audience of their peers. Since this is an activity giving directions, the most salient response will probably be to make the directions as complete and as detailed as possible. If this is the case, have students write "completeness" or "descriptive words" or exciting verbs after the "How?" at the top of their paper. Explain that, when they begin revising the papers, this is the specific focus of this revision. They should concentrate on making their papers as complete and detailed as possible. (Caution them, however, not to overdo description or use of particular words.)

6.   Give the students sufficient time to add to their pieces until they feel the works are complete.

7.   If the paper topics happen to be descriptions of activities the students can do in the classroom, they can evaluate themselves by exchanging papers and trying to carry out the instructions exactly as they are written. The places where classmates do not understand what to do next are the places where the authors need to provide more information. Students can be given more time to do further revising based on classmates' reactions.

8.   If time permits, ask the students to write another draft of the directions so that they can be read by younger children (6- to 7-year-olds). To do this, repeat steps 4, 5, and 6. The "what" answer will remain the same, but the "who" will be whichever age group you decide upon. To answer the "how" question, ask the students to brainstorm all the things that they think make writing readable to young children. Again as a class, they should decide on the one or two criteria they've listed that seem most important ("short sentences" or "easy words," for example). Students should write these points at the top of their papers after the "How?" and should incorporate these specific recommendations into their papers as they revise. If younger students are available, they can be brought in to test the effectiveness of the revisions in the same way that the previous revisions were tested according to classmates' performances.

9.   Continue to work on revision for different audiences, emphasizing varying levels of sophistication and complexity in language, content, and emphasis of informa-

tion. A possible assignment is to have students write two versions of a short persuasive or explanatory essay on the same topic to two different people (a friend and the school principal, or a grandparent and a sibling, for example). Afterwards, discuss with students how their versions differ and why.

A sample essay would be: Pick a classmate you think would make a good student-council representative and explain in a letter to a friend why you chose that person (or why you want your classmate to support your choice). Now write a letter to your school principal explaining your choice.

Notes

1. Some of the suggestions for *revision practice* are not appropriate for practicing planning, use of resources, or special formatting/presentation of work. For instance, short, focused assignments are easier for students to revise, but don't lend themselves to practice with the planning sheet or to students' creative impulses with alternative formats. Alternating shorter, more targeted writing assignments with longer, more complex ones should enable students to practice adequately all aspects of the writing process.

2. *Audience* is an essential aspect of writing, and many students never fully grasp its importance. One of the trickiest aspects of audience for a student is where the teacher fits in. Most assume that all papers are written for the express purpose of satisfying the teacher's burning desire to read about Iceland (or whatever the topic may be)! And in some ways, this is true: The teacher *is* the target audience of students classroom writing efforts.

    But in other ways, the teacher should *never* be the students audience. Why not? Because students must learn to write for *their own* purposes and enjoyment. As long as students think that writing assignments are to be done merely to please their teachers, they will never grasp the broader relevance of good writing, nor learn the pleasure of writing well. Granted, to succeed academically, students *must* bear in mind the teacher's requirements and preferences. On the other hand, students *must* write to be informative, entertaining, and interesting—both for themselves and for *any* reader.

    You might share with students some anonymous examples of past years' students' work that is technically correct but dull, or not perfect grammatically but lively and readable. Let them in on the truth: Teachers are human, and while they value academic precision they also value a good read and an original approach. Teach them to be their own audiences—one way is to get them in the habit of sharing their papers with the class as a whole or with classmates in revision groups. Another way is to encourage them to infuse their writing with their own interests and ideas. Then they will learn how to read their own (and others'!) writing more evaluatively and with more interest.

Connections

Reading Lesson 2.2: Differences in Kinds of Reading and Reading Strategies

Reading Lesson 2.6: Re-Reading

Follow-Up Activities

1. Each week (or as often as possible) give students a short writing assignment and ask them to revise it. Continue to use the revising recipe, giving students some freedom in deciding what to write for the "how" section.

2. As often as possible, use writing assignments for which students can receive tangible responses (arguments convincing you that they need a field trip or a math-free day; letters to raise money or solicit submissions for a class publication like a newsletter; friendly letters to pen pals; business letters to companies suggesting a change in a product or a new idea).

LESSON 3.7 **Choosing a Format**

Central Themes

Knowing Differences

Knowing Process

Synopsis

Activities designed to give students practice in working with different report formats, and to demonstrate the value of re-working information into their own words. The activities are followed by a list showing the students different types of formats for written reports that they can choose from during the school year.

What To Do

1. Prepare copies of the following handout (from the Student Handout section):

    • "Alternative Formats for Writing Assignments"

2. On the first day of this activity, hand out a page of simple information about a common topic (the weather, cockroaches, the flu). After reading time, have your students, make a quick poster on the topic (see description of "Learning Poster" following).

3. On the second day, ask students to get out the information sheet from Day 1 and do a short interview on the topic (e.g., interview a cloud or a roach).

4. On Day 3, have students write a short obituary on the topic (the demise of a hurricane, a memorial for Matilda the Roach).

5. On Day 4, discuss with students the purpose of these slightly bizarre assignments. The most important point to make during this discussion is that by having to shape the same information to fit different formats, students should begin to achieve a fuller understanding of the material, and should be less inclined (or able) to copy. Focus on the issues of "ownership" (truly understanding, in their *own* terms, new information on a topic), and copying, by asking the following sorts of questions:

    • What do you think was the purpose of working on the same topic three times, a different way each time?
    • What did you learn?
    • How often did you have to go back over the information sheet?
    • How well do you think you'll remember the information now?
    • Was it hard? Was it harder than doing a straightforward, written report on the topic?

- Which parts were most enjoyable?
- Was it tempting to copy?
- What makes you want to copy?
- How well do you have to know the information to copy?
- Were there parts or times when you couldn't copy?
- How well do you remember things that you've copied?

6. Now that the students are aware of the basic point of this lesson, it's time to get them interested in, and excited about, different formats for written reports. Samples of several types of formats are provided at the end of this lesson. Hand out copies to the students, and explore the formats as a class. Encourage your students to try one or more of the formats described whenever they have a report to do. In choosing a format, students should take into account their own interests as well as the nature of the topic. Add your own examples of different types of formats to the list if you wish. Examples include:

Alternative Formats for Writing Assignments

Non-Fiction Children's Book

After researching any field of interest (choice may or may not be left to the student), the students need to rewrite the text and make it suitable for a first- or second-grader. The steps involved include:

1. researching
2. creating rough-draft text in a simplified manner
3. illustrating
4. combining rough draft sketch and text
5. making a good final copy
6. binding
7. displaying in the library, in a classroom for younger children (to observe their reaction), or in own classroom for others to read.

Crossword Puzzle

Use a normal crossword format. (Your school may have computer programs that generate crossword puzzles when given definitions and clues.)

Original Quiz

After researching a topic, students make up their own quiz for classmates, parents, or teachers. They need to supply the answers and the reasons for the answers on a separate page. Emphasize that answers must fully explain the questions. A simple yes or no won't do. The students can pick from a variety of question formats (true/false, multiple choice, essay, or fill-in-the-blank).

Tour Guide (with written instructions)

Somebody has to have the job of informing the unsuspecting public where it is they are about to go. Have your students produce a map with reference points. They have to write an explanation for the locale of each reference point. This format should be limited to a short, enjoyable way of condensing information.

Encyclopedia Article Not Based on an Encyclopedia

Make the topic something they won't find in an ordinary (or any) reference book. Insist on two sources of information. The following are some possibilities:

oral interview

magazines

notes from TV or radio programs

first-hand observation

phone calls to resource people

on-site visits

letter-writing

Have students write their report based on information from these sources. Use an encyclopedia entry as a model for the form of their reports.

Political or Propaganda Pamphlet

After researching a current-events topic, students create a short political or informational pamphlet. Highlights, pictures, and brief background information all can go into it. The purpose is to convince readers to support a politician or a particular opinion on an issue.

Learning Poster

Students have to present their research in an attractive, eye-catching format. The writing is used to illustrate the graphics, and vice versa.

Time Line

Students organize information chronologically along a time line that they create. This works well on biographies as well as the usual history topics.

Acrostic

Either you or your students pick a topic and/or materials. The report format is an acrostic of their researched topic.

Interview with a Famous Figure

The student writes a mock interview with a character from history after doing research into his or her life.

Comic Strip

The student uses information from research to create an illustrated comic strip.

Letters Between Historical Characters

The student writes letters between two historical characters corresponding with each other, using the background and lingo of their times.
  Some guidelines for the student:

1. After doing research, jot down at least 5 important pieces of information from the source(s).

2. This list should be used as a guide. Make sure that you include details about each of these pieces of information in the letters.

3. Write two letters. Person 1 writes a letter to Person 2, who then writes a letter back to Person 1. One of the letter-writers must be a "real" character from the source(s) used for the report. The other can be made up, or also a character from a research source.

4. The letters should somehow indicate the time and place in which they were supposed to have been written.

Obituary

For biographical research reports, students can write an obituary column for the local newspaper.

  (This handout was developed by Toby Caplin and Dan Klemmer.)

7. Once the students have reviewed the list, discuss:

    - Which formats interest you the most? Why?
    - Which formats do you like the least? Why?
    - Which formats go better with which subject areas? Are there some types of formats that seem better matched to an English report, while others are better for science?
    - Choose the best report format (in your opinion) for each of the following subject areas: English, social studies, math, science, music/art. (Add examples of subjects from curriculum.)
    - Does using different types of formats make doing reports easier, more fun, more interesting?

Connections

Writing Lesson 3.2: Using Past Experiences in Writing

Writing Lesson 3.3: Getting Down to Work

Reading Lesson 2.2: Differences in Kinds of Reading and Reading Strategies

Homework Lesson 4.6: Making It More Interesting and Personal

Follow-Up Activity

For the next written report assigned to the class, insist that each student choose a format unlike the standard report. Have the students present their reports to the class, or at least describe their report formats if there is too much material to cover. Ask the class to comment on how interesting the formats are to them and why.

LESSON 3.8 Using a Variety of Resources

Central Themes

Knowing Differences

Knowing Process

Synopsis

An activity and discussion designed to show students the diversity in available sources of information, the fact that many sources are interesting and fun to pursue, and the relevance of specific sources to specific subjects.

What To Do

1. Ask the students to name as many different sources of information as they can think of. If they need help, start them off by suggesting that a textbook is a source of information. List responses on the board.

2. As a class, determine how many different kinds of sources have been listed. Many (perhaps most, or even all) may turn out to be printed matter (books, newspapers, magazines) or sources of printed matter (libraries, bookstores).

3. Now lead students to consider more unusual resources:

   - Does this list include any people? What kind of person could be a source of information? Does a person have to be a "certified expert" to be a source of information? (Polling and oral histories are two important sources precisely because they do not consult "experts.")
   - Does this list include any places? What kind of place might be a source of information (travel destinations, museums, stores, factories, historical sites)? Does a place have to have printed materials available in order to be a source of information?
   - Does this list include any "things" that are not printed matter? What kinds of things could be considered a source of information (any artifact: an arrowhead or a collection of old photos; movies; artwork; television programs)?

4. As a class, brainstorm another list of sources of information. This time try to focus on sources that are not composed largely of printed matter. The list might include:

   - your mom
   - an old graveyard
   - an archaeologist at the local college
   - a moon rock
   - a foreign embassy or consulate

- an old record album
- your oldest living relative
- a neighbor who immigrated to the United States
- any museum (sports museum, transportation, natural history)

5. Once the brainstorm is over, go over the list and ask students to explain why they think the items are sources: What could you find out from each? (e.g., Your mom might be a source of information about what life was like when she was your age or about what is involved in running a household. A really old graveyard might be a source of information about how long average lives used to be, or what kinds of names were popular years ago.)

6. To make the point more forcefully, you might ask students to reflect on times when they actually encountered alternative sources of information:

- Who in the class remembers a field trip they took?
- Where was it, and how was that place a source of information?
- Does anyone ever remember having a guest speaker in the classroom?
- How was that person a source of information?
- Has anyone ever brought an object into class to use as a source of information (an aquarium, a pet)? What was it, and what information did it provide?

7. Explain to the students that using alternative sources requires information-gathering techniques perhaps different than they are used to. When you get information from the encyclopedia, you just pull out a volume and read the article about your subject—not much of a challenge. But getting information from other sources is more like detective work. You have to poke around a little, ask a lot of questions, jot down clues, and consult as many different sources as you can. It takes more imagination than just reading one article, but it's also a lot more interesting. The encyclopedia isn't a waste of time, though—often it's the first place to look to find out about *other* possible sources of information.

8. Choose a current topic on which a written assignment will be based. Have each student think of or locate three possible sources of information, and write how they would realistically go about getting information from these sources. For example:

- Schedule an interview with local person or expert.
- Write to a distant person or organization and ask for a written or taped response to a written interview.
- Visit a local site, take pictures, and gather available literature.
- Write for information about a distant site.
- Consult a reference librarian.
- Rent a pertinent video and take notes.

9. As a class, share ideas and discuss other ways of getting information from a variety of resources. Questions to consider:

- What if you are studying an ancient civilization? Since what you're studying happened so long ago, are you restricted to sources like books and articles? What kinds of people, places, or things could you consult if your topic is ancient?
- If you do schedule an interview with a person, what will you need to think about, or do, before actually conducting the interview? Examples: Is the person just going to talk? Are there any questions you specifically want answered? How will you remember what the person says? Will you take notes? Tape the interview? What if you can't get to the person? Could a telephone interview work?

10. Finish the lesson by asking the students to help you list the benefits and problems of using a variety of sources. Talk with students about how to solve or minimize the problems students anticipate.

Connections

Writing Lesson 3.3: Getting Down to Work

Homework Lesson 4.5: Resources

Follow-Up Activity

Have students keep a running list in their journals of all the resources they use. Suggest that they use a point or star system to highlight the resources they find most helpful or personally like using. Are there resources they would like to use but have a logistical problem accessing? Discuss these last items as a class, looking for helpful suggestions.

Student Handouts

For *Lesson 3: Getting Down To Work*
- Planning Sheet for Writing Assignments
- Susanna's Writing Plan

For *Lesson 4: Getting Unstuck*
- Writer's Block and Other Problems Worksheet
- Writer's Block Scenarios

For *Lesson 5: What's the Point of Revising?*
- Paragraphs Needing Revision
- Revising for Clarity: A Recipe

For *Lesson 7: Choosing a Format*
- Alternative Formats for Writing Assignments

Susanna's Writing Plan

Directions

Use the information provided about Susanna to design a plan to help her get her writing assignment done well and on time.

Susanna's Assignment

Write a two-page report on some aspect of the life or writing of the author Mark Twain. The report is due in one week.

Susanna's Writing Profile

Susanna doesn't mind writing but
1. never knows how to begin her papers.
2. is not sure where to make her paragraphs.

Susanna's personal interests are traveling, dancing, and animals.

Susanna likes to do her writing at home in her room.

Susanna likes to give her own opinions in her writing.

Susanna has read *Tom Sawyer*, a book by Mark Twain.

Susanna likes speaking in front of the classroom and making other people laugh.

Make a writing plan for Susanna using the writing plan handout.

PLANNING SHEET

Teacher Requirements:
  Subject:
  Kind of project:
  Length:
  Due date:
  Other guidelines:			

Ideas & Possibilities:	1	2	3
Possible topics			
Connections with personal interests previous projects			
Possible resources			
Possible modes of presentation			

Feedback notes

Writer's Block and Other Problems Worksheet

What I was working on when I got stuck

When and where it happened

How it felt

Tricks I used to get unstuck and whether they worked

Writer's Block Scenarios

Directions

Help the following students overcome writer's block by analyzing why they are having problems and suggesting what they can do to get unstuck.

Student 1: Ed

Ed is writing a one-page science paper about how the human heart works. It is due in two days. He just finished reading in his science book about the heart, but already he can't remember what it said. He looked *heart* up in the dictionary, but it didn't say very much. His parents aren't at home, and now he's just sitting in his room listening to music. What can he do?

Student 2: Tasha

Tasha has to write a five-line rhyming poem for language arts class. It is due tomorrow. The poem can be about anything Tasha wants. She wrote the first line, "My bike can go so fast," but then she got stuck, and she's been trying for ten minutes to think of what to do next. Now she feels really angry and doesn't want to work on the poem any more. What can she do?

Student 3: Chris

Chris has to write a summary of the major events of Abraham Lincoln's life. He has one week to write the summary. His teacher told him to look up the information at the library or at home, but he doesn't have a library card, and his family doesn't have that kind of book at home. Chris is really interested in Abraham Lincoln, but he figures he can't do this assignment because he can't get the information. What can he do?

Paragraphs Needing Revision

Directions

Help these students revise their paragraphs to improve their writing. Check for spelling and grammatical errors. Do you think the sentences are in a good order? Can anything be left out? Is anything unclear? Should more information be added? What would you change, and why?

1. My house in the woods. There is a big yard, well kind of big, in front, and a hill in the back. We go there a lot in the diferent sesons of the year but mostly in the seson of July. It is made of bricks and wood and has a bunch of rooms. It smells sometimes. The house is in New Hampshere. I think it has six rooms, not counting the bathroom.

2. I went to a concert and saw madona. It was awesome, there were maybe 20,000 people there. She sang alot of her songs, like "Papa Dont Preach and Cherish." She was realy great, and her dancers were realy great too. It was an awesome show. Wicked awesome!!!! Id go again.

3. My favorite subjeck is math because in math you get to use numbers and you don't have to read a whole lot and its pretty easy I think. Social studies is OK too but sometimes boring. Math is best I don't mind science but sometimes it is too hard because I don't understand all the words and so I can't understand what things mean. English is the worst it is too hard.

Revising for Clarity: A Recipe

Directions

If you have ever used a recipe or tried to assemble something using directions, you know that if the instructions are not clear, it's very confusing! This recipe needs revision. Decide where it is unclear and rewrite it so that it makes more sense.

Scottish Shortbread Pan Cookies

Ingredients: 2 cups sifted flour

baking powder

salt

1 cup soft butter

½ confectioners sugar

Sift together flour, baking powder, and salt. Mix butter with sugar until very light and fluffy. Mix in flour. Refrigerate. Put chilled dough into pan. Bake 20–25 minutes. Cut while warm.

Alternative Formats for Writing Assignments

Non-Fiction Children's Book

After researching any field of interest (choice may or may not be left to the student), the students need to rewrite the text and make it suitable for a first- or second-grader. The steps involved include:

1. researching

2. creating rough-draft text in a simplified manner

3. illustrating

4. combining rough draft sketch and text

5. making a good final copy

6. binding

7. displaying in the library, in a classroom for younger children (to observe their reaction), or in own classroom for others to read.

Crossword Puzzle

Use a normal crossword format. (Your school may have computer programs that generate crossword puzzles when given definitions and clues.)

Original Quiz

After researching a topic, students make up their own quiz for classmates, parents, or teachers. They need to supply the answers and the reasons for the answers on a separate page. Emphasize that answers must fully explain the questions. A simple yes or no won't do. The students can pick from a variety of question formats (true/false, multiple-choice, essay, or fill-in-the-blank).

Tour Guide (with written instructions)

Somebody has to have the job of informing the unsuspecting public where it is they are about to go. Have your students produce a map with reference points. They have to write an explanation for the locale of each reference point. This format should be limited to a short, enjoyable way of condensing information.

Encyclopedia Article Not Based on an Encyclopedia

Make the topic something they won't find in an ordinary (or any) reference book. Insist on two sources of information. The following are some possibilities:

> oral interview
>
> magazines
>
> notes from TV or radio programs
>
> firsthand observation
>
> phone calls to resource people
>
> on-site visits
>
> letter writing

Have students write their report based on information from these sources. Use an encyclopedia entry as a model for the form of their reports.

Political or Propaganda Pamphlet

After researching a current-events topic, students create a short political or informational pamphlet. Highlights, pictures, and brief background information all can go into it. The purpose is to convince readers to support a politician or a particular opinion on an issue.

Learning Poster

Students have to present their research in an attractive, eye-catching format. The writing is used to illustrate the graphics, and vice versa.

Time Line

Students organize information chronologically along a time line that they create. This works well on biographies as well as the usual history topics.

Acrostic

Either you or your students pick a topic and/or materials. The report format is an acrostic of their researched topic.

Interview with a Famous Figure

The student writes a mock interview with a character from history after doing research into his or her life.

Comic Strip

The student uses information from research to create an illustrated comic strip.

Letters Between Historical Characters

The student writes letters between two historical characters corresponding with each other, using the background and lingo of their times.
    Some guidelines for the student:

1. After doing research, jot down at least five important pieces of information from the source(s).

2. This list should be used as a guide. Make sure that you include details about each of these pieces of information in the letters.

3. Write two letters. Person 1 writes a letter to Person 2, who then writes a letter responding to Person 1. One of the letter writers must be a "real" character from the source(s) used for the report. The other can be made up, or also a character from a research source.

4. The letters should somehow indicate the time and place in which they were supposed to have been written.

Obituary

For biographical research reports, students can write an obituary column for the local newspaper.

(This handout was developed by Toby Caplin and Dan Klemmer.)

CHAPTER 4

Homework Planning and Execution

Tina Blythe, Noel White, Jin Li, and Howard Gardner

Contents

Homework Themes

1. Knowing Why
    - Understanding the purposes for homework.
    - Relating homework to other work in and out of school, now and later.
2. Knowing Self
    - Recognizing current homework practice.
    - Identifying personal strengths and weaknesses in terms of homework.
3. Knowing Differences
    - Knowing the homework requirements for different classes.
    - Understanding the different kinds of homework and the different approaches that are appropriate for each.
4. Knowing Process
    - Getting organized.
    - Knowing and using resources.
    - Incorporating one's interests, talents, and experience into the work.
5. Reworking
    - Understanding the purpose of reworking homework.
    - Developing strategies for going over homework and checking for errors.

About the Homework Chapter

It is possible for students to have difficulty with homework *even if* they understand the academic part of the work—for instance, how to divide fractions or how to spell tough words. Students may not have had the opportunity to develop the practical skills they need, such as how to organize their time and how to use resources. The ideas in this chapter should help students to build the practical abilities needed for homework.

The Five Themes

Lesson 1 emphasizes "knowing why."

Lesson 2 emphasizes "knowing self" and "knowing differences."

Lesson 3 emphasizes "knowing self," "knowing process," and "knowing differences."

Lesson 4 emphasizes "knowing process."

Lesson 5 emphasizes "knowing process" and "knowing differences."

Lesson 6 emphasizes "knowing self" and "knowing process."

The theme of "reworking homework" is not covered directly in a lesson, but is best addressed by revisiting parts of lessons where students need more help, by giving the same assignment more than once if students have trouble with it, and by reviewing difficult homework in class. Because students may not change their homework habits quickly, try to spell out the PIFS themes in concrete situations to provide opportunities for them to practice as frequently as possible.

Overview of the Lessons

In **Lesson 1**, students discuss the purposes of homework, an activity that students normally are not engaged in voluntarily. This discussion prepares them for subsequent lessons in the chapter.

Lesson 2 asks students to identify their personal homework habits and needs in order to begin recognizing their areas of strength and weakness.

Lesson 3 provides a number of activities designed to help students learn strategies from, as well as offer tips to, others for better homework practice.

Lesson 4 presents students with a case study. Through examining and discussing this case, students learn about the importance of organization (a central skill in homework) and develop strategies for organizing their own homework.

Lesson 5 is designed to alert students to the variety of resources they can use to enhance their homework practice—resources often overlooked by students.

In **Lesson 6**, students are encouraged to make their homework more interesting and personal by incorporating their own talents, interests, and experiences in and out of school. In learning to take control of their own learning, students can become empowered and motivated.

Suggested Teaching Sequence

Although the lessons are numbered, you might want to change their order to accommodate your regular curriculum. For instance, if you prefer to get students settled into particular routines at the beginning of the year, you might want to consider teaching Lesson 4 (a routine to organize oneself) and Lesson 6 (a routine to adapt homework to one's interests) first.

LESSON 4.1 Purposes for Homework

Central Theme

Knowing Why

Synopsis

A brief discussion on the purposes for homework.

What To Do

1. Conduct a class discussion about the purposes for homework. You might want to use some (or all) of these questions:
    *   Why do we do homework at all?
    *   How does homework change as you get older? Why?
    *   What would school be like without homework?
    *   What can you learn from doing homework?
    *   Can you think of anything that you do that is like homework?
    *   Can you think of anything that adults do that is like homework?

2. Write students' answers on the chalkboard. After enough discussion time to elicit a variety of responses, ask students to review some of the main themes of the discussion. (They might do this by categorizing the class's responses.)

3. Ask students to identify among their responses the ones that indicate how homework can be important for more than just learning subject matter. Emphasize that doing homework builds responsibility and skills (similar to practicing for sports or rehearsing for a play) that will be helpful in adult life.

4. Optional: Allow five minutes for students to write in journals about their most important reasons for doing homework.

Connections

Introduction Lesson 1.1: Why School?

Testing Lesson 5.1: Why Tests?

Follow-Up Activities

1. Each time students do a homework assignment, ask them to write the goal(s) at the top of their paper. (Once they have finished the assignment, you might also ask them to evaluate briefly how well they've met that goal.)

2. Return to this discussion (and to what the students have written in their journals) after completing the lessons in the Homework chapter—or in a couple of months, whichever is later. Ask students to think about if and how their ideas have changed about the purposes for homework.

LESSON 4.2 **Knowing Your Personal Needs**

Central Themes

Knowing Self

Knowing Differences

Synopsis

Students consider their personal homework needs and set goals for themselves.

What To Do

1. Prepare copies of homework questionnaire either A or B from the Student Hand-outs section. (Both A and B ask basically the same questions: A provides a more structured format for answering; B leaves more room for students to answer in their own words.)

2. Ask students to answer all the questions on the homework questionnaire.

3. On another day, have students review their answers. Briefly brainstorm as a class by asking students to name some of the different things that go into doing home-work successfully. Keep track of responses for everyone to see. (Responses might include: going to class, taking notes, getting the assignment, bringing the right book home, arranging time to work, having a place to work, keeping papers and materials organized, staying on track, remembering to bring the assignment back to school.)

4. Encourage students to think about how homework differs from class to class. For example, social studies homework may involve going to a library to gather infor-mation for a report—something almost never done in math.

5. When finished listing responses, arrange them into a few broad categories (for ex-ample, preparing, being organized, doing the work, handing in work).

6. Ask students to think, based on the discussion and their questionnaires, about what aspects of homework are important to them. Have each student make a list of things she would like to improve and ideas on how to begin making improve-ments. Have students record their lists in their PIFS journals.

7. As appropriate, encourage students to think about what they do *well* either in homework or in something that might be related, such as practicing a sport. Ask them to consider how they might build on that strength.

Connections

Introduction Lesson 1.4: Puzzle Challenges

Reading Lesson 2.3: Personal Reading Profiles

Reading Lesson 2.4: Strategies for Thoughtful Reading

Writing Lesson 3.3: Getting Down to Work

Writing Lesson 3.4: Getting Unstuck

Follow-Up Activities

1. Have the class make a display of "Helpful Homework Strategies" to remind them of their own best ideas.

2. Have students fill out a homework questionnaire again later in the year. They can compare their responses to see if their strategies have changed or improved.

LESSON 4.3 **Personal Solutions to Homework Difficulties**

Central Themes

Knowing Self

Knowing Process

Knowing Differences

Synopsis

An experience (three different possibilities are described) to expose students to the materials and methods available to help them with homework difficulties.

What To Do

Choose one of the following three activities.

A. Homework Fair

1. Designate a period of time as a "homework fair" devoted entirely to helping students figure out ways to overcome difficulties that they have with homework.

2. Ask students to identify important areas to consider by reviewing their homework questionnaires and their plans for improvement (from Lesson 2).

3. Set up (or have students set up) homework displays around the room. For example: exhibits of helpful homework materials (trapper keepers, daily-planner notebooks, pocket folders, etc.); motivational displays (a chart showing how many hours each basketball star practices free throws); demonstrations of personal progress (before-and-after stories). Since good displays require much preparation, you might rely on students to do the work. Preparation for the fair can be a class project; or you might ask individual students to prepare displays or presentations that explain their particularly successful ideas.

4. Walk students through the displays, explaining whatever may be unclear (or have students do so for displays they've created). Allow students to talk to each other about their reactions. If it is difficult to have students walking around the room, you might pass materials around as you discuss them.

5. Include a "workshop" as a part of the fair. Have a table or some space for students to make their own materials, or to personalize purchased materials.

6. Require that each student write down at least *two* new ideas he learned from the fair. At the end of the fair, have students read the ideas aloud and tell how they can be used to solve their own problems.

B. Field Trip to a Supply Store

1. Arrange for students to visit a school- or office-supply store. If possible, arrange for a store representative to present some of the materials available there that can help students with homework (notebooks, resource books thesaurus and dictionary, folders, pencils, pens, highlighters).

2. Let students know that they'll be going to a store to see some of the materials that can help them better handle homework. Ask students to prepare by reviewing their homework questionnaires (from Lesson 2) and lists for improvement.

3. Visit the store with your class.

4. Sometime around when you visit the store, include time in class for students to make their own materials or to personalize purchased materials.

5. Require that each student make a note of at least *two* new and useful things (strategies or materials) she learned. At the end of the trip, have each student share the things he noted (reading aloud) and tell how these things can be used to solve his own problems.

C. "Dear Abby"

1. Ask students to review their homework questionnaires (from Lesson 2) for ways in which they get stuck or have difficulty doing homework.

2. Have students write letters in the style of "Dear Abby" to ask for advice on how to handle a particular difficulty. For example, "Dear Abby, the teacher always tells us to show our work on math problems. So I do, but then she complains that she can't find my answers because the paper is too messy. Is this fair? What should I do?" Or, "Dear Abby, I always think I understand my writing assignment until I get home and try to do it. Then it doesn't make any sense. Help!"

3. Have students exchange letters and write responses to each other.

4. Have students read their letters aloud and comment on the advice they get from their partners: How useful is it? Will they try to use it?

Note

Whichever option you choose, make sure that students consider whether their solutions to homework difficulties are appropriate for different kinds of homework (long-range assignments, overnight math worksheets, defining vocabulary).

Connections

Introduction Lesson 1.5: Individual Differences in School

Reading Lesson 2.5: Troubleshooting While Reading

Testing Lesson 5.10: Summarizing Testing Strategies—Writing a Testing Handbook

Follow-Up Activity

Have students record in journals the new and useful ideas, tips, or materials that they discover. Later they can revisit what they've written and consider how they've used what they learned or (if appropriate) why they *haven't* used what they learned.

LESSON 4.4 **Organization**

Central Theme

Knowing Process

Synopsis

A demonstration/discussion to help students understand the importance of organization and begin developing helpful ways for organizing their work.

What To Do

1. Find or prepare a striking example of disorganization (such as a disorganized folder created by you or borrowed from a willing student, an overflowing desk, or perhaps a diagram or photo of a messy desk). Also have on hand copies of an extremely disorganized piece of student work.

2. Display this example of disorganization for the class. Discuss the pros and cons of such a beast. For instance, it's easier to throw homework anywhere into a messy folder than to place it in the right section, but when you need to find it later. . . . If you want to take the time, the class might actually work on reorganizing the mess.

3. Ask students if your example of disorganization looks familiar. In what ways are they disorganized? (Examples might come from school or outside of school.)

4. Either demonstrate, describe, or ask the class to think of how organization is important *outside of school* (for example, labeling files of important records, keeping records of expenses, having a sports or personal calendar). What would a disorganized baseball player be like? What kind of organization is involved in throwing a good birthday party? Encourage students to think about how some of the strategies learned in school (particularly through having to keep up with homework) can apply elsewhere.

5. Shift the discussion toward *solutions* or examples of *good* organization. Discussion can be most helpful if students show concrete examples (both good and bad).

6. Pass out copies of the disorganized student assignment to the class. Divide students into groups of two or three. Have them organize the messy work and rewrite it. To guide their work, you might write some questions on the board:

- What is wrong with this assignment?
- How would you help the student who did it to reorganize this mess?
- Why do you think your way is a better way to organize?

7. Have students share their work. Ask each of the groups to show their reorganized sheet and to explain how their version is better than the one you distributed. Stress the important organizational strategies that come up (for example, numbering items, putting math calculations on a separate sheet if they're not part of the assignment, lining things up, taking the perspective of the reader/teacher when checking work). Jot these strategies down on the board and have students write them in their journals.

Connections

Writing Lesson 3.3: Getting Down to Work

Reading Lesson 2.3: Personal Reading Profiles

Testing Lesson 5.4: The Process of Taking Notes

Follow-Up Activities

1. Whenever you can, use yourself to demonstrate how organization is an important life skill. Point to times when being organized helps you. And, when you find yourself having difficulty due to *disorganization* (such as missing an appointment that you didn't write down, or forgetting papers at home), confide in students. Ask them to help you think of ways to avoid such problems.

2. Periodically, when you come across examples of student work that is particularly well organized, share the examples with the rest of the class—if the students who did the work don't mind. (Unless you have an opportunity to recognize everyone's work at some point, you might want to avoid identifying who did it.) Be sure to spend some time explaining why and how the work exemplifies good organization.

LESSON 4.5 **Resources**

Central Theme

Knowing Process

Knowing Differences

Synopsis

A brainstorm on resources to use when doing homework in different subjects.

What To Do

1. Collect two sets of tools and resources. The first should be various everyday items: a hammer, a measuring cup, a road map. The second group should be examples or representations of the resources that can help students to do homework in your subject.

2. Introduce the concept of resources as those things around us that we use all the time to help make decisions or get something done. Show as examples the hammer, ladle, or whatever you have available.

3. Ask students what they might use to help them build a skateboard, make a meal, or perform any appropriate activity with which they are familiar.

4. Suggest that, as they do in everyday life, resources can help with homework. Solving math problems, doing research, writing essays, reading literature, or doing any kind of homework without using resources would be like a mechanic working without wrenches, gauges, or manuals. The job just wouldn't get done.

5. Ask students to consider an upcoming or a recent assignment, and have them brainstorm all of the different resources they could use (or did use) to help with that assignment.

6. As students name a resource, display an example or a representation of that resource.

7. If you have examples of a wide range of resources, keep them hidden until named, and challenge students to try to name all of the resources you have brought.

8. When finished with the list, as time permits, discuss how particular resources can be used at home for various kinds of assignments.

9. Give a homework assignment that requires the use of resources. Ask students to use at least two resources that they normally don't use. Have them record resources that they thought of but couldn't find, as well as ones they actually used.

10. When students have completed the assignment, discuss their resources in class.

   • Who had the most unusual resource?
   • What was the most *helpful* resource?
   • Who thought of resources they couldn't find? Why couldn't they find them?
   • What problems did they encounter in using resources?
   • How might they solve those problems next time?

Connections

Reading Lesson 2.5: Troubleshooting While Reading

Writing Lesson 3.4: Getting Unstuck

Writing Lesson 3.8: Using a Variety of Resources

Follow-Up Activity

Each time students do a homework assignment (or periodically), ask them to record at the top of their paper any resources that they use. Occasionally, in class, review some of the resources that students report using. Have students share what they've found most and least helpful for different kinds of assignments.

LESSON 4.6 **Making It More Interesting and Personal**

Central Themes

Knowing Self

Knowing Process

Synopsis

Demonstrations and discussion to help students consider the importance of making homework interesting both for an audience and for themselves.

What To Do

1. Have on hand two items: a piece of work that is perfectly comprehensible but deadly dull (such as a scene from a poorly made documentary, or a videotape of a very boring presentation of a student project); and another piece of work that is as interesting as the first one is dull.

2. Ask your students to watch or read the work you've decided to use. Let them continue until you see them losing interest.

3. Ask them to describe the way the work was presented and to give opinions on it.

4. Show the second, more appealing piece. Ask them to make comparisons. If they were to re-do the first, boring work, how might they enliven it?

5. As a class, list kinds of assignments that students *can* approach in interesting, personalized ways, and kinds of assignments that students *cannot* approach in such ways.

6. Ask students to consider the open-ended assignments, such as papers and projects. Lead a discussion about ways of making such work more interesting for an audience and for oneself:

    *   What kinds of homework assignments have you done?
    *   How might you have made those assignments more interesting for someone else, such as a teacher, to read or look at?
    *   Imagine a student who has to write a report about an American president. The student hates writing reports, but loves football. How might he make the report more interesting to write?

- Given your own strengths and interests, what might you add to your work (drawings, graphs for written assignments, unique methods of presentation involving acting or music for oral work)?

Connections

Introduction Lesson 1.3: Sharing Talents

Introduction Lesson 1.5: Individual Differences in School

Writing Lesson 3.2: Using Past Experiences in Writing

Writing Lesson 3.7: Choosing a Format

Follow-Up Activity

In subsequent homework assignments that allow room for different approaches, encourage students to make their work both neat *and* interesting.

Student Handouts

For *Lesson 2: Knowing Your Personal Needs*, and *Lesson 3: Personal Solutions to Homework Difficulties*

- Homework Questionnaire A
- Homework Questionnaire B

Homework Questionnaire A   Name_____

Directions

Put a check mark next to the answers that best describe you (you can check more than one), or add your own answers if necessary.

1. Where do you like to do homework?

    ___inside

    ___outside

    ___in a large, open space

    ___in a small, cozy space

    ___other: _____

2. When do you do your homework?

    ___in school

    ___right after you get home

    ___before dinner

    ___after dinner

    ___no fixed time, whenever I have time

    ___other: _____

3. What is the mood of the place you learn best?

    ___warm and friendly

    ___cool and businesslike

    ___other: _____

4. What do you do if you get stuck or don't understand part of the assignment?

    ___I try to figure it out myself.

    ___I ask my parents or siblings to help me.

    ___I call my friends.

    ___I quit.

    ___other: _____

5. How fast or slow do you like to work on homework?

    ___slow, with plenty of time to think

    ___at a steady pace

    ___fast, to get it done

    ___other: _____

6. What makes you want to do homework?

    ___when I think up my own work

    ___when I can learn something

    ___when someone makes me

    ___when I am working for a reward

    ___other: _____

7. What do you do to plan the time you spend on homework?

    ___I don't plan my time at all.

    ___I estimate how long it will take to do the work.

___I do some things at the same time every day or week so that these things begin to happen without thinking about them.

___I write in a calendar or on a schedule when things need to be done.

___In my head I plan my time but I don't keep track of plans.

___other: _____

8. How do you decide that your homework is ready to be handed in?

___when it's finished

___after I go over it and check for errors

___I read the assignment and go over my answers again; if I see errors I will redo the work.

___I just hand in whatever I did even if I didn't finish it.

___other: _____

9. Next to each statement mark whether it happens to you "a lot," "sometimes," or "never."

My homework is not labeled or has no name._____

I don't have time to do my homework._____

I don't feel like doing homework._____

I try, but can't get my homework done on time._____

I forget my homework._____

I don't know there is an assignment until it's too late._____

I don't have what I need to do the work at home._____

My assignment is not neat enough for the teacher._____

I don't have time to check my work before handing it in._____

I don't feel like checking my work before handing in._____

10. Describe something good about the way you handle homework:

11. Describe a "trick" or "shortcut" that you use to save time on home-
     work:

12. Describe something *not* very good about the way you handle home-
     work:

Homework Questionnaire B   Name_____

Directions

Answer the following questions.

1. Where do you like to work? Explain why.

2. When do you normally do your homework? Explain why.

3. Describe your homework environment (anyone else in the room? noise? music?).

4. What do you do if you get stuck or don't understand part of the assignment?

5. When do you work quickly? Slowly?

6. What kind of homework do you enjoy? Explain why.

7. What kind of homework do you dislike? Explain why.

8. On nights when you have more than one assignment, how do you decide which assignment should be done first?

9. Do you go over your homework and check for errors once it's finished? Why?

10. Next to each statement mark whether it happens to you "a lot," "sometimes," or "never."

My homework is not labeled or has no name._____

I don't have time to do my homework._____

I don't feel like doing homework._____

I try, but can't get my homework done on time._____

I forget my homework._____

I didn't know there was an assignment until it's too late._____

I don't have what I need to do the work at home._____

My assignment is not neat enough for the teacher._____

I don't have time to check my work before handing it in._____

I don't feel like checking my work before handing in._____

11. Describe something good about the way you handle homework:

12. Describe a "trick" or "shortcut" that you use to save on homework:

13. Describe something *not* very good about the way you handle homework:

CHAPTER 5

Preparing for and Using Feedback from Tests

Wendy M. Williams and Robert J. Sternberg

~~~~~~~~~~~~~~~~~~~~~

Contents

Testing Themes

1. Knowing Why
   - What are the roles of tests in and out of school?
   - How does testing relate to other class work?
2. Knowing Self
   - Recognizing current study strategies and test-taking practices.
   - Identifying personal strengths and weaknesses in terms of testing.
3. Knowing Differences
   - Recognizing different kinds of tests and test questions, within and across subjects.
   - Knowing what each test can and cannot determine about the test-taker.
   - Knowing different strategies that are appropriate for each test.
4. Knowing Process
   - Understanding that long-term preparation is necessary when preparing for tests.
   - Knowing both long-term and short-term strategies for test preparation, as well as strategies for solving problems during actual test-taking.
5. Reworking
   - Using the results of tests as an opportunity for self-reflection and a stepping-stone toward more productive learning and test-taking.

About the Testing Chapter

Tests make many students uncomfortable. To these students, tests represent the mysterious moment of judgment when their "real ability" is measured. No wonder test-taking becomes a tense and dreaded experience!

In reality, tests are no more than an attempt to measure approximately a student's comprehension of a domain of knowledge. It is essential for teachers to determine whether students are assimilating required material—and tests represent one reasonable approach. However, it is important to remember that tests are only *one* way to gain insight into students' ability and comprehension. All teachers are familiar with students who do poorly on tests, but perform remarkably well on in-class demonstrations or home-prepared projects. Many students become so unnerved by the test-taking process that they do not perform up to potential. These same students shine in other domains of performance.

Although tests are not always the most effective way to gauge students' abilities, it is clear that we are unlikely to get rid of tests in the short run. Therefore, it is important to recognize that students have difficulties with tests, and to help them do as well as they can, given the situation.

The ideas in this chapter are intended to stress that tests are simply one measure of performance among many that students encounter throughout their lives. School's paper-and-pencil tests are appropriate indicators of ability in some ways and inappropriate in others. By placing tests in their proper perspective, the activities in this section can help students to approach tests more calmly and effectively.

The Five Themes

Lesson 1 emphasizes "knowing why."

Lesson 2 emphasizes "knowing self" and "knowing process."

Lesson 3 emphasizes "knowing self" and "knowing process."

Lesson 4 emphasizes "knowing process."

Lesson 5 emphasizes "knowing self," "knowing differences," and "knowing process."

Lesson 6 emphasizes "knowing differences" and "knowing process."

Lesson 7 emphasizes "knowing differences" and "knowing process."

Lesson 8 emphasizes "knowing self" and "knowing process."

Lesson 9 emphasizes "reworking."

Lesson 10 emphasizes "knowing why," "knowing self," "knowing differences," "knowing process," and "reworking."

Overview of the Lessons

Lesson 1 deals with the importance of, and reasons for, tests. Comparing and contrasting familiar (and perhaps less threatening) extracurricular tests with tests given in school can help students both demystify tests and acknowledge their importance. Understanding what tests can and cannot measure is a first step toward students and teachers using tests more effectively.

Students must come to see that tests measure what they have learned all along—not merely what they have crammed the night before. They can't study for tests very well if they haven't paid attention in class. **Lesson 2** stresses the importance of a solid foundation of information built through careful listening to, and understanding of, information presented in class.

Lesson 3 addresses the importance of taking notes. Although critical to success in school, notetaking seems to many students an onerous and fruitless task. A clear demonstration of the value of class notes, and some comparisons with the notes that students make effortlessly outside of school, should help to ease the sense of drudgery that often characterizes school notetaking.

Simply understanding the importance of notetaking won't ensure that students take better notes. They'll need specific advice, techniques, and many opportunities for practice. The process of taking notes is the focus of **Lesson 4**.

Memory is a murky and elusive concept for many students. Often they believe that they should know something if they see or hear it once. Or memory has a magical quality: Either information will "stick" in their minds or it won't. Understanding memory helps students see themselves as being in control of their minds and their test performances. **Lesson 5** guides students in developing a general idea of how memory works, a feeling for the different kinds of subject matter for which memory is important, and a sense of their own optimal modes of recall.

Students should recognize that there are different types of test questions, and that there are different strategies for approaching questions of different types. The goal of **Lesson 6** is to help students recognize which types of questions are easy for them, which are hard, and how to compensate for those difficulties.

Paying close attention in class and taking good notes are important aspects of preparing for a test, but especially important are forethought about the content of the test and an understanding of one's own best ways of mastering that content. **Lesson 7** details these points and others as it covers the process of studying for tests.

Lesson 8 again addresses testing, but focuses on troubleshooting problems during the test itself. Students' grades on tests reflect not only their knowledge of the subject matter but also their ability to perform in a testing situation. For many students, tests are emotionally stressful. Fear or tension causes them to "freeze up," preventing them from showing what they really know. Often tests impose a time limit that is uncomfortable for students, and seeing even familiar material in unfamiliar formats can be disconcerting. Anticipating such problems and planning for them can help students take control of the difficult situation and make the best of it.

Learning how to accept and use feedback on performances is a task we face repeatedly throughout our lives. Graded tests are the feedback that students receive most regularly—and probably that they least enjoy. A graded test can provide the student with a wealth of information about how well she studies, what kinds of test questions she answers best, and what she can do to improve her performance on the next test. But too often, students only glance at the grade on a returned test, not understanding—or even ignoring—the opportunity to learn more about themselves. And too often, teachers do not use the returned test as a teaching tool. **Lesson 9** emphasizes how teachers can help students use feedback from tests to develop good testing strategies, as well as strategies for general classroom learning.

Lesson 10 gets students involved in the actual writing and production of a "testing handbook" by having them put in tangible form, for themselves and others, what they have learned about preparing for, taking, and using feedback from tests. The production might stretch out over a week or two, but should prove well worth the time as students put together otherwise disparate bits of information.

Suggested Teaching Sequence

The sequence of lessons is not fixed. Infusion of the lessons into existing curricula is encouraged, as is the revisiting of lessons. Teachers should feel free to revise lessons as necessary.

Acknowledgements

Melanie Gordon Brigockas, a researcher at Yale University, contributed to the follow-up activities. Lessons 3 and 4 on notetaking were developed and drafted by Dan Klemmer, a fifth/sixth-grade teacher in Cambridge, Massachusetts.

LESSON 5.1 Why Tests?

Central Theme

Knowing Why

Synopsis

Discussions designed to encourage students to develop a sound understanding of the role of tests both in and out of school.

What To Do

1. How are tests used outside of school? Ask students if they ever get tested outside of school. Although their initial response might be a resounding *no*, press them a bit.

    - Do any of you play sports? How do you know when you're getting good? Could games be like tests?
    - Have you ever given a musical performance for which you had to prepare?
    - What about the first time your parents or older siblings gave you a certain privilege or special task (watching younger siblings, taking care of a pet, staying home alone)?
    - Have you ever been given a new chore or a job working for a neighbor?

    Might these instances be tests of students' sense of responsibility and trustworthiness? Encourage them to come up with more test-like situations from their extracurricular lives and list these on the board. Virtually any situation that involves performing or demonstrating something that has been practiced can count. As you compile the list, discuss the following questions:

    - What purposes did these tests serve?
    - How did you tell whether your practicing had been done correctly?
    - How did you know whether you had done well?
    - Did you learn anything about how to do it better next time?

2. How are tests used outside of school in adults' lives? Ask the students to list occupations and roles (airline pilots, police officers, teachers, doctors, truck drivers) for which testing is necessary. You might also have students break up into groups and see which group can come up with the most occupations. Pick out a few of the occupations they have suggested and talk about the following questions:

    - Why do we test these people?
    - What do people in these occupations need to be good at (what would they need to be tested for)?

- What sorts of tests might people in these occupations be given to see if they have the necessary skills?
- What could happen on the job if these people were not tested?

You might also discuss with them the less formal tests that adults encounter every day. A teacher teaching a class, for example, is undergoing a kind of test, as is the firefighter confronting a burning house. The process of applying for a job is also like taking a test. Share with the students some of the everyday tests that you go through, how you get feedback about your performance, and how that feedback helps you to make plans for future situations.

3. How are tests used in school? Ask students to list the sorts of tests they take in school. Discuss with them a series of questions like the ones listed in item 2:

- Why are tests used in school?
- What do tests tell teachers? Parents? Students? How can they use this information?
- Do some subjects lend themselves to testing more readily than others (math versus English; science versus art)?
- What would school be like without tests? (Ask for both pros and cons.)
- Would you feel uncomfortable not knowing what your grades and academic standing are?
- What might happen in school if students weren't tested?

4. Finally, ask students to compare the list of school tests with the two lists of outside-school tests. How are the lists different? How are they the same? The most obvious distinction is likely to be that most of the tests on the school list are written, and customarily receive a number or letter grade. On the other hand, many of the tests on the outside-school list will be "performance" assessments, in which the test-taker actually demonstrates a particular skill and is judged accordingly (perhaps pass-fail).

5. Ask students to think about testing situations that involve both a pencil-and-paper component and a performance component: driving tests, CPR certification tests, auto mechanic exams, surgeons' evaluations. What does each half of the test tell about the test-taker? If they were only given written tests (or only performance tests), what would be left out? Then ask students to think about school pencil-and-paper tests in this light: What can and can't they measure? Get concrete examples here. A spelling test, for instance, might demonstrate how well you can memorize, but won't show how well you can use a dictionary. A timed math test might show how quickly you can add and subtract, but won't tell how resourceful you can be in figuring out how to do a puzzling problem.

There are three important points to make from all of these discussions:

- *Tests aren't simply a school phenomenon.* They are an omnipresent part of life, so it makes sense to think about how to do them well and how to use them to advantage.

- *Tests are sources of information, not just stamps of success or failure.* Just as an altimeter reading lets a pilot know whether his plane is too high or too low, performances on tests can tell students what they know well, what they need to put more work into, and what kinds of tests and test questions they're most likely to have trouble with—or do well on. (Forthcoming lessons will help students get better at "reading the altimeter.")
- *Tests can provide important information about students' progress in acquiring certain skills and knowledge, but often they measure only a part of that progress.* Different kinds of tests yield different kinds and amounts of information about achievement; students vary in how they best display their knowledge. Some do well on in-class tests, others on take-home essays. Some shine on short-answer quizzes but can't perform well on long multiple-choice tests. No student is perfect, but neither is any test.

Connections

Homework Lesson 4.1: Purposes for Homework

Follow-Up Activity

Ask students to think how homework is a form of testing. Have them list the ways homework can work like a test and how they can benefit from it. Have them also list ways homework cannot serve the same purpose as tests—why it is not always a good substitute. Ask students if they would like to have take-home tests occasionally in place of in-class tests.

LESSON 5.2 Active Listening in Class

Central Themes

Knowing Self

Knowing Process

Synopsis

Activities designed to help students improve their test preparation by learning material carefully and completely from the day it is introduced. The activities provide an opportunity for students to learn some skills used by effective listeners, including self-monitoring, self-evaluation, reviewing information, and reformulating information in their own words.

What To Do

1. Pose a few imaginary situations. What if they were going to take part in a sports tournament—but didn't practice until the night before? What if they had to take the road part of the driving test without ever having driven a car? What if they had to sing a song in front of an audience but didn't start to learn it until the morning of the performance? (Or, have they ever had a dream in which they had to perform in some way—but were completely unprepared?) How would they feel as they were getting ready to play, or drive, or sing? What would the actual performance be like? What should they have done to get ready? Students can also describe some actual times when unpreparedness got them in trouble.

2. Explain that taking a test for school is similar to those situations in at least one respect. If students want to do well, they usually need to start preparing long before the actual test—the same way that baseball players start spring training in February, although the season doesn't start until April. Tell the students that paying attention in class is an important first step in preparing for a test. Explain that they'll be working on some ways to do this better.

3. What follows is a list of techniques and activities to help students become more conscious of listening in class. Pick the ones that seem the most workable to you and use them systematically during the next week or two of classes (perhaps a different one for each day, or a different one every two days). You might also list the activities on the board and let the class vote on which ones to try.

    • *Soft Points.* During a normal class discussion or lecture, slip into the dialogue the statement, "Tally one soft point." Don't change the tone of your voice as you say it. Students who are listening will notice and will make a mark each time it is said.

Students who are not listening will not know to make the mark. (Watch for students who pick up on the visual cue of seeing other students move to mark the tally, making their own mark with a slight delay. If this occurs, allow those students to give themselves ½ point.) At the end of the period have students calculate their percentage of soft points gained for the period. These can be used for students to measure their own listening growth from day to day. (A good place for students to make the marks is on the top righthand corner of their note sheets.)

- *Fingers in the Air*. At appropriate breaks in the lesson content, stop and ask for a "reading" from the students about the level of meaning they have acquired. Simply ask, "May I have a reading, please?" Students hold up one, two, or three fingers to show their level of understanding:

    One finger = not understanding the material
   Two fingers = understanding some material or not confident of understanding
  Three fingers = material is meaningful and understandable

    Scan the room and decide how best to proceed. If lots of students do not understand, some backtracking might be needed. Even if most students signal "three," you might want to probe with some questions to determine if they do indeed understand.

- *Say-back or write-back*. After introducing each major concept, stop to ask students to say or write what they understood. For say-back, call on individual students to say in their own words what they understood. Ask the rest of the class if they agree with the summary. Students who disagree must give a reason, and state their own understanding. For write-back, all of the students take a moment to write a short sentence summarizing their understanding. Take this chance to walk about the room and scan students summaries. Again, you might have a few students read out loud and ask others to respond, or you can collect summaries and read them anonymously.

    Note: For say-back or write-back, be careful to stress that the exercise is designed to help develop listening skills—not to test or embarrass particular students. Set the example for the class both by using a supportive, nonjudgmental approach to correcting errors in understanding, and by requiring other students to use the same approach when evaluating their peers' responses.

- *Cross-examination*. At appropriate intervals, stop the class and ask students to write one question they have about the material. These should be genuine questions about points that they want to understand better. In small groups, students can share their questions and decide which ones they can answer and which ones they cannot, given the information covered so far. You might also collect these questions at the end of class and use them to help plan the next day's activities.

- *Self-chart*. Ask students to stop and reflect on the quality of their listening at pre-set intervals. Set a kitchen timer to an interval tolerable to you and agreed upon by the class (perhaps every ten minutes). When the bell rings, the student thinks to himself, "Was I listening?" and marks his chart with a yes or no. (A less intrusive option is for you randomly to generate the interruptions yourself, by verbally interrupting the flow of the lesson.) At the end of the period, students add up their marks and compute the percentage of times that they were paying attention. They can also keep daily records for several days to see if they can improve their "yes" score. (Note that you'll need a timer and the students will need a place to keep their tallies.)

4. After introducing and trying each method, ask the students to record a short evaluation in their journals. Did they like using this method of active listening? Did it help? Why or why not? When all methods have been tried, ask the students to agree as a class on the one or two that worked best. Again, encourage the students to explain why they liked certain methods more than others and why they think the method they chose will work best. Continue to use the chosen methods on a formal and regular basis. (If there are some students for whom the chosen methods don't work, encourage them to use on their own the ones that did work for them.)

Connections

Testing Lesson 5.3: The Importance of Taking Notes

Follow-Up Activities

1. Ask students to think of other ways to test listening skills or to help make someone a better listener.

2. Ask students to keep a journal of what is going on in class when their concentration starts to break down. What is the topic? What type of lesson is it—lecture, class discussion, demonstration, video presentation? Are there distractions in class that are diverting their attention? For instance, are they tired or mentally preoccupied, perhaps with a test coming up in the next class or a game after school? Tell students the purpose of this exercise is to look for a pattern so they can predict future listening lapses and work to avoid them. Ask them to keep track of successes they have in avoiding lapses.

LESSON 5.3 The Importance of Taking Notes

Central Themes

Knowing Self

Knowing Process

Synopsis

An experiment and discussion to illustrate the use of notetaking, both in school and out.

What To Do

1. Start with a demonstration to get students thinking about the value of notes. Divide the class in half, and tell one group to take notes and the other group just to listen as you read a passage containing factual information relevant to the week's material. Review the important parts of the passage with the class, then continue with business as usual.

2. Later in the day, have students put away their notebooks and quiz them on the material you read earlier. If you like, give the notetakers a chance to look at their notes for a minute or two, prior to the quiz. (Tell everyone it's only an experiment and not to panic!) After the quiz, compare the recall of the notetakers and the listeners-only. You might have them exchange papers and grade one another. Once the papers are scored, tally in two columns on the board the scores of notetakers and listeners-only. Discuss the results.

3. After this exercise, ask students to list examples of how adults use notetaking in their jobs or leisure time. Possible examples include carpentry measurements, architectural or building blueprints, scores and statistics at sports events, journalistic interviewing, court stenography, or police investigations.

4. Now ask them to look at their own lives. When do they take notes outside of school? If the students seem stumped, you might begin by naming phone-call messages and shopping lists as everyday examples. How about writing down the name of a song or group the students heard on MTV, or an 800 number for a concert ticket giveaway? Have students name other examples of notes taken outside of school. The physical task of writing down information in these examples should seem reasonable to the students, and connecting these to notetaking might unlock some students' paralysis in the classroom.

5. To encourage students to take notes during an instructional period, emphasize the connection between *notetaking* and taking a *telephone message*, the sort of note they

probably make most frequently. When teaching, you might want to refer to notes you want taken as "phone messages." This will take the edge off the task, and a little humor can go a long way: "Ding-a-ling . . . Phone call for Room 303: When you divide fractions, invert and multiply."

Connections

Testing Lesson 5.2: Active Listening in Class

Testing Lesson 5.5: Understanding Your Memory

Writing Lesson 3.1: Writing in School and Out

Follow-Up Activities

1. Have students make a list in their journal of times when they or someone they know didn't write something down and later regretted it. Remind them that there are many reasons for not writing things down: You didn't think it was important enough at the time; you thought you would be able to remember the information; you didn't have time; you didn't feel like it; or you didn't have a paper and pencil. Ask students to target their most common reasons for not writing things down, especially those times when they come out the loser. Then have them reevaluate their personal profiles, incorporating their weaknesses in this area and suggesting ways to overcome them.

2. Tell the class in anecdotal style about some delicious-sounding food you made, reciting to the class the ingredients and how to combine and cook them. Make the recipe one of moderate complexity that the students might be excited to try out themselves. Do not, however, give them the opportunity to write down what you are saying. Keep to the story format. Then, after some time and another activity have intervened, ask students to write down the recipe you recited earlier, perhaps offering some small reward or incentive to anyone who can reproduce it correctly. The students will be surprised at how something they thought would be easy to remember just isn't.

LESSON 5.4 The Process of Taking Notes

Central Theme
Knowing Process

Synopsis

Activities and discussions designed to demonstrate methods for improved notetaking.

What To Do

1. Tell the class they'll be working on improving their notetaking ability. Point out that taking notes is a highly individual practice. Some students seem to need notes more than others, but *all* students need good notetaking skills to survive in school and later on in life.

2. Open the discussion of notetaking techniques by emphasizing that taking good notes is *not* simply a process of *copying* information! Good notetaking involves *deciding* what is important and writing it down in a way that makes the information *relevant* and *useful*. Good notes let you reconstruct what you read or heard, keeping the original meaning intact. *Organization* of the information is key to taking good notes.

3. Introduce the concept of *key words*. Students need to see that notetaking can be a task that is quick and fairly easy to do. A note can be a single word that stands for and generates recall of a greater amount of information. Identifying the right key words takes practice with a variety of subject matter. Begin the practice of identifying key words by reading single sentences of information and asking students to identify the key words. For example:

    -   If *Auntie Mame* calls, tell her that her *car* has been *towed*.
    -   Today will be *warm* and *rainy*. Highs will be near *70°F*, with occasional glimpses of sun.
    -   *Food* is mixed with *enzymes* in the *small intestine*. The enzymes *change food into molecules* that *cells* can *use*.

    Continue with more examples from different subjects. You might let the students try making up some sentences for the rest of the class to key word. Test the usefulness of key words by having students return to them at the end of class to see if they can reconstruct the original sentences' meanings.

4. Introduce the concept of *highlighting*. When working with texts that are long and complex, finding key words becomes more difficult. Here's where highlighting

comes in. Highlighting is the process of identifying important passages in written material. For example, the first time students read a chapter in their textbook, they can highlight (using read-through markers), or underline, any passage that strikes them as important. They can then review only the highlighted passages and pick out the key words in each. These key words are the ones that go into notebooks for use in reviewing. You might want to point out to students here that highlights can be long and wordy and, by themselves, not very helpful for learning material or reviewing quickly before a test. Highlighting needs key wording to make it useful.

5. Photocopy or write a passage on an overhead transparency and give the same photocopied passage to each student. (This could be the opening few paragraphs in a homework assignment for that night.) As a class, you can decide what needs highlighting, and then which words qualify as key words. As you mark words on the transparency, students can mark them on their own papers. Have students finish the reading, highlighting, and key wording for homework, and then complete the exercise on the overhead the next day, using students' suggestions from their own work.

6. Tell students that they can also use diagrams and drawings to summarize material. Ask students for examples of when this approach would work best. Examples might include the structure of objects (such as cells, pieces of furniture, types of trees), spatial descriptions (directions to a place, travel plans), or time-based information (time lines, histories, cycles).

7. Now that you have pointed out several different ways of approaching notetaking, stress the fact that we all have favorite notetaking strategies. Some of us are verbally oriented and like to use just words. Others are visually or spatially oriented and like to use outlines and drawings or pictures. There are three basic ways of taking notes:

- summaries of words in sentences
- outlines of words showing the order of meaning and interrelationship of parts
- pictures or diagrams

Model these for the students based on one particular reading passage or filmstrip. *Show* the three approaches and how they work.

8. Ask the students which way they prefer. Now ask which way they think would best prepare them for a multiple-choice science test, an English essay test, a math test, and so on. Remind the students always to take into account both *their own preferences and abilities* and *the subject matter and purpose for the notes* (type of test) when choosing a notetaking approach.

9. Summarize all of the above information on the chalkboard as follows (pointing out that you have key-worded the directions for them):

- *Read* the article to get a *general sense* of what the article is about and to *highlight*.
- Re-read the highlighted passages and *key words* to focus on *important details*.
- If appropriate, use *drawings* to summarize information.

10. Have students practice notetaking using material that is relevant to one of this week's lessons. Distribute copies of a passage and ask students to practice highlighting and key wording. Once they have finished, have them compare highlighted passages and key words with classmates in small groups or as a class. Have them defend their choice of key words. Do the exercise yourself and describe your own process to the students.

11. Simply taking notes won't magically improve students' work. The notes must be understandable (not to mention findable!) when it comes time to study. Discuss with students how they can keep their notes usable over the course of the semester. Some suggestions:

    - Underline or number important words.
    - Skip lines between topics.
    - Keep separate, clearly labeled notebooks for different subjects.
    - Rewrite sloppy notes.

Notes

Highlighting. Of course, highlighting or underlining text in school-owned textbooks is not usually feasible. Photocopies are good for practice, especially if all students are working to highlight the same passage. Many schools also have discard textbooks or magazines that students can use for practice. However, if a school-owned text is the only option, the highlighting can be done by laying pieces of sticky-pad paper in the book to mark the passage. Key words can be written down in notebooks, rather than circled in the text.

Length of Lesson. This is a long lesson, and it should be taught over a few days so students can absorb the material.

Connections

Reading Lesson 2.2: Differences in Kinds of Reading and Reading Strategies

Homework Lesson 4.4: Organization

Follow-Up Activity

Once students have begun to take notes with key words and highlighting on a regular basis, have them use their key words to reconstruct the original passages after several days or even weeks have passed. If they compare their reconstructions to the original passages on a regular basis, they will begin to develop a sense of the level of notetaking detail they need to preserve meaning.

LESSON 5.5 Understanding Your Memory

Central Themes

Knowing Self

Knowing Differences

Knowing Process

Synopsis

Discussions, journal writings, and a demonstration to help students understand memory and how to use it to advantage.

What To Do

1. Discuss repetition in daily life and how it works to instill particular messages. Show the students that they have memorized many songs word for word and many commercials from television as a function of repetition (sometimes more repetition than they would like!).

2. Ask the students the following questions. Have them write down answers in their journals before sharing them with the class:

    • How many times do you think you have to go over something to remember it?
    • Have you ever had the experience of not being able to remember something, and then when it is said, thinking, "Oh yeah, I remember that"?
    • Why do you think teachers make you write your spelling words five times?
    • How do you store your memories: in pictures, in words, in the way something felt, or through some other method of your own?
    • Which kinds of test questions are the hardest for you?

3. Ask the students to consider whether memorizing is uniformly useful across subjects and content areas. How important is memorizing to math? Science? Language arts? Music? Ask whether memorization would be an effective technique for studying for an essay test on a short story, compared to a multiple-choice science test. Students should realize that memorization is extremely important in some areas, but less important in others.

4. Model memorizing something for the class yourself (such as the middle names of five students). Carefully repeat the names aloud to yourself until you are able to say them all smoothly. If you are more visually oriented, write the names on the chalkboard, or describe the sorts of images you call to mind to help you remember. You might also try making up a mnemonic. Then take away your prompts and try

to recall the names. Emphasize for the class the importance of taking care at first because it is possible to memorize words the wrong way in the first place.

5. Review the following memorization strategies with the class. These strategies work best with memorizing lists. Use your judgment regarding your students' readiness to absorb these strategies. Omit any that are too complex.

- *Rehearsal.* Simply repeating information over and over again in the order given (most commonly used strategy).
- *Categorical clustering.* Grouping things together by category. For example, suppose you have to learn a list of vocabulary words such as *robot, trend, survivor, trespass, recommend,* and *settle.* Try memorizing by category: *nouns* (robot, trend, survivor) and *verbs* (trespass, recommend, settle). Another possible set of categories is *r-words* (recommend, robot), *t-words* (trespass, trend), and *s-words* (survivor, settle). Make sure you know the number of categories you have memorized, so that if one is missing, you will realize it.
- *Interactions Within a List of Words.* Suppose you have to learn about important events in colonial Boston. Your list includes *Paul Revere, the Boston Tea Party, Old North Church, the Boston Massacre,* and the year *1776.* Try making mental images in which items on your list interact with each other in a way that sticks in your memory. For example, picture *Paul Revere* drinking *tea* at a *party* in *Boston.* He leaves the *tea party* in *Boston* to walk *north* to an *old church.* Outside the *old church,* he sees *1,776* birds flying over people lying *massacred* in the street.
- *Method of loci (places).* In this memorization strategy you visualize walking around an area you know well. Along this walk there should be landmarks you know well—your own home, a park, a store, and so on. At each landmark you imagine an interactive image between the word you're memorizing and the landmark. So if you are trying to learn the names of the planets in our solar system in order from the sun, you might start at your home, picturing the *sun* shining right over it. Then move in your mind to the next building, with *Mercury* over it. The next building will have *Venus* sitting on top of it, the one after that will have *Earth* above it, and so on down the line of your street.
- *Acronyms and Acrostics.* These strategies depend on a verbal approach instead of imagining something in your head. An *acronym* is a word in which each letter stands for another word. Consider this list of math terms: subtract, divide, add, multiply, equals. The first letters of these words can form the acronym DAMES—an easy way to remember the list. An acrostic is similar except that you make a sentence rather than a single word to help remember the new words. In this case, the sentence could be, *My silly dog eats apples.*

To give students one real-world example of how people memorize important information, tell the class about a person who always memorizes important or frequently used telephone numbers because he knows he will either lose the written number or not have it at hand when he needs it. Years will go by and he will never forget the written number. What's more, he will use this system for his own number so she can give it to people and be pretty sure they will remember it too, even if they don't write it down.

His number now is Idaho 57. His children call home on an 800 number that ends with "Hug Sami" (Sami is their cat). He knows there are other ways he could solve the problem of having a number when he needs it, but for him this works particularly well.

6. Assign a memorizing task (preferably one related to your curriculum), having the students work in pairs to quiz each other. You might have students memorize the spelling of new words, a verse of poetry, a list of math formulas, or a few science definitions. Instruct students to count the number of repetitions it takes them to memorize. Then test their memory. If needed, have them repeat the material more times (adding to total count) until it can be recalled easily. Let the class know that there will be a "memory check" on the information another day.

7. Before the end of the period, have students describe the memorization process in their journals. How many times did they need to repeat? What sorts of prompts helped them to memorize: A visual image? An association with something familiar? Setting the words to a well-known tune? Ask students to share some of their tricks and encourage them to try out any of their classmates' methods that sound interesting.

Connections

Testing Lesson 5.3: The Importance of Taking Notes

Testing Lesson 5.7: Studying for an Upcoming Test

Introduction Lesson 1.4: Puzzle Challenges

Follow-Up Activities

1. Each time students need to memorize something, encourage them to look in their journals at their list of memory techniques and pick a new one to try. Have them mark the ones that seem particularly useful and identify the kinds of material for which they work best.

2. Challenge the students to invent a special memorizing system that could work for them in notetaking for school or in something else they do. Have volunteers share successful strategies with the class.

LESSON 5.6 Understanding Test Questions

Central Themes

Knowing Differences

Knowing Process

Synopsis

An activity to show students the importance of understanding test questions.

What To Do

1. Ask students to list all the different kinds of test items that they have encountered in the past. Keep track on the chalkboard, and have the students compile lists in their journals. The kinds of items might include multiple choice, essay, fill-in-the-blank, short answer, matching, and true-false.

2. Ask each student to record in her or his journal the two types of questions that are the hardest and the two that are the easiest for her or him to answer. Call on some students to share their answers.

3. Next, ask the students *why* they think certain types of questions are hard or easy for *them*. Show that different students have different reasons for preferring certain questions.

4. Pick a few of the questions that many students described as particularly difficult. Ask the class to generate reasons for putting these types of questions on tests. What do they show? What information do they contain? Even truly tough questions are given for very good reasons, and figuring out those reasons might lead to a strategy for answering them. Students may say that questions that require them to explain their reasoning are difficult. You can point out that such test questions can occur in every subject. Why do teachers like this sort of question? Also, why is it that sometimes the answer alone—even if it is correct—is not enough?

5. Ask the students to make up three or four sample test questions relevant to a current class topic, with each question being of a different type. Let students volunteer to read one question to the class. Have the class respond with comments regarding what is good or bad about each question, how easy the question would be to study for, and any other comments.

6. Discuss the sorts of questions they might find on tests in different subjects. What sorts of questions are they likely to find on a math test? English test? Social studies

test? For example, a test on a short story might require students to generate anwers not found specifically in the story. Opinion questions require them to support their interpretations with examples from the works, but there are no strictly "right" or "wrong" answers to these types of questions. In contrast, most questions on a math test are much more straightforward and do have a single "right" answer.

7. Pick a particularly tough question from each subject area and discuss how the students might go about trying to answer each one.

8. Discuss the following *strategies for answering test questions* with the students:

    - Read the directions! Often students assume that they know what the test calls for, but sometimes important clues and information are explained in the directions. If you skip them, you may be answering questions incorrectly without knowing it.
    - Plan your time. If the test has three sections, glance over each part briefly and make yourself a mental note (or a written note in the margin) about how much time you should allot to each section. Look at the clock and tell yourself at what time you should start each new section.
    - On multiple-choice questions, you often can find out the correct answer by using the process of elimination to get rid of incorrect options. Even if you don't know the answer at first, you may still be able to figure it out by considering all alternatives.
    - Always *guess* on tests even if you aren't sure. You will draw on your knowledge and you may be right. Don't give up because you're not sure! Some types of questions will be scored with partial credit—you might get some points if you guess. On multiple-choice questions, you might be 100% right.
    - Test questions are often organized roughly in order of difficulty. This means easier questions come first and harder ones come later on. If you have more trouble with questions further along in the test, that's probably normal. If you have lots of trouble with any of the first few questions, however, you might be reading into the question or looking at it from the wrong point of view.
    - Sometimes test questions are worth different amounts of points. It is to your advantage to be sure to answer the questions that are worth the most points, given the amount of time and effort they will require. Don't start on a 50-point question that will take 10 minutes to answer when you only have 3 minutes left, though!
    - On hard questions, don't go with your first reaction. Take the time to *consider alternatives* and think it through, whether it's multiple-choice, essay, or whatever. Ask yourself what the teacher had in mind. Try to think like the teacher to see if the most obvious answer might be wrong. On the other hand, don't overdo it and worry that every question is a trick question. That's unlikely!
    - Don't give too much time to any one question. Mark it and return to it later if there's time. Don't forget about it!
    - Don't avoid questions that look difficult—they may be easy for *you*. Read them carefully and give them a chance.

- Break long questions up into parts for easier handling.
- If there is time, check over your test when you think you're finished to make sure you haven't skipped, or forgotten to return to, a question.

Connections

Introduction Lesson 1.4: Puzzle Challenges

Reading Lesson 2.5: Troubleshooting While Reading

Follow-Up Activity

Before each test, walk the class through study strategies appropriate to that form of test, using actual content material that the students must study.

LESSON 5.7 Studying for an Upcoming Test

Central Themes

Knowing Differences

Knowing Process

Synopsis

Some small-group activities, a case study, and discussions to help students identify and refine their personal strategies for studying for tests.

What To Do

A. Before the Lesson

1. Prepare copies of the following handouts (from the Student Handout section):
    - "A Case Study of a Student Preparing for a Test"
    - "The Test Log Sheet"
    - "Preparing for Tests" (This handout summarizes test preparation tools and strategies discussed so far. It can accompany this lesson or Lesson 10: Summarizing Testing Strategies—Writing a Testing Handbook.)

B. Anticipating the Content of the Test

1. Explain that figuring out what will be on the test is probably the most important step in good preparation. When a substantive test is nearing, use this activity to help students check their perceptions of which information is testworthy. Split the students into small groups. Have them create review sheets for the upcoming test. Encourage the students to talk about potential items and to reach a consensus about which are important enough to be included.

2. Have the groups use their review sheets to make up potential test questions. They should try to make the questions like the ones they think you will write. When groups are finished, collect their questions, redistribute them to different groups, and have the students answer them. Students should be instructed to give feedback

to the designing group regarding the content of the questions, as well as the likelihood that you would actually ask questions like this.

3. Now ask students how they decided what information would be on the test. What clues did they use? What clues might they have used? How did they know what kinds of questions to make up? The list might include hints that you gave in class ("This is important," "Be sure to notice"), outlines and boldface words in the textbook, their own highlighting and key wording, or notes in their notebooks that they marked as particularly important.

C. Strategies for Studying

1. Having established ways of picking out the important information to study, help students to think about their study strategies. Distribute the handout, "Case Study of a Student Preparing for a Test" (also reproduced here). As a class, analyze this case study of one student's preparation for an upcoming test. Read the scenario to the class while the students follow along using their copy. Then ask for feedback about how good or bad the student's strategies were and why. Questions at the end can guide discussion.

Case Study of a Student Preparing for a Test

Tom, a sixth-grader in Ms. Washington's introductory algebra class, has a math test on Friday. Ms. Washington announced the test on Monday, and Tom wrote it down in his notebook. By Tuesday night, Tom was worried about the test. He didn't think he understood the material very well. He tried to do some extra problems, but grew frustrated and closed his book. He decided to watch TV before going to bed. "I have all Wednesday and Thursday to study anyway," he assured himself. "I need to relax now."

On Wednesday night, Tom grew more and more nervous about his test. He did all his other homework first, so that it was late by the time he got around to studying algebra. Tom realized that he was tired and couldn't concentrate very well. He quickly looked over the chapters and then went to bed. He said to himself, "I'll just do some problems tomorrow and then I hope I'll be able to get it. I'm too nervous and tired to work now."

On Thursday in class, Ms. Washington went over the material that would be on the test. When she asked if anyone had any questions, Tom thought to himself, "She'll think I'm stupid if I say that I'm having trouble with this stuff. I'll just figure it out myself tonight."

By Thursday night, Tom was panicked. He was so nervous that he had a hard time sitting still. He fidgeted with the pages of his textbook and tapped his pencil nervously on his desk. He tried to do some problems, but found he got stuck in the same place every time. Frustrated, he looked up the answers in the back of the book. Then he put his books away, saying, "Oh well. I'll bet nobody else understands this either. Maybe the test will be easy anyway. Yeah, I just have to hope it will be easy."

- How do you think Tom did on the test? Why?
- What study strategies did Tom use or try to use? (He wrote the test down as soon as it was announced; he intended to study a little each night for three nights in a row.)
- Was he successful in using any of them?
- What specific strategies might Tom have used to prepare better for his math test?
- What type of studying should Tom do to prepare for a math test?
- If the test had been on a short story, what different strategies might he have used? Why?

2. Ask students to list in their journals the test-preparation strategies they use now or have used in the past. Tell them to star the ones that they think work best, and to write an "X" next to the ones they don't think have helped much.

3. Ask each student to write down (anonymously, if they prefer) on a small piece of paper one test-preparation strategy he or she has used in the past. Collect these sheets. Read examples aloud to the class, and solicit comments on each strategy— what's good about it? What's bad? Allow students to submit other strategies for discussion as they think of them.

D. Recognizing Differences in Tests

1. Remind students that tests in different subjects often have different kinds of questions (Lesson 6). This suggests that they would study differently for a math test than for a science or an English test. Break the class up into four or five small groups and assign each group a content area. Instruct each group to list strategies that would be particularly good for their subject. Have a spokesperson from each group read the list to the rest of the class and keep track on the board of the similarities and differences between subject matters. Make sure the lists include the following strategies, which you should discuss with the class. Encourage them to find ways to make the studying more fun for themselves, by relating the subject matter to their own interests or by making up games (a few examples are provided).

- *Math tests.* Re-read chapters and review notes carefully; review homework. Memorize formulas and practice problems. Pretend the numbers refer to an important telephone number or combination lock. Pay attention to details. Check your answers to be sure they are correct, and practice some more if they are not.
- *Language arts tests.* Re-read assigned material and notes carefully; review homework. For literature or poetry, read for general meaning, character, plot, action, and theme. For vocabulary, memorize definitions and spellings, and practice using the words in interesting sentences, or a short sports broadcast, or a concert review. For grammar, memorize the rules and review examples in your text or notebook.
- *Social studies tests.* Re-read chapters and notes and review homework. Read both for a general overview of the topic and also for learning relationships between

specific events. Memorize important facts (Who? When? Where?) you will need for short answers and to support your essays. Pretend that you are the teacher and you will have to teach this information to the class.

- *Science tests*. Re-read chapters and notes both for a general overview of the topic and what it means, and also for learning terms, definitions, and relationships between details. Go over labs and homework assignments. Memorize definitions and formulas. Make up a matching game to help you memorize.
- *In general*. Multiple-choice and short-answer questions require more specific knowledge within an area, while essay questions require an overview of an area.

E. Reflecting and Recording Study Strategies

1. Begin a procedure to be used for the rest of the school year. Hand out the Test Log Sheets that you have prepared. On these the students should note the dates of their tests, the kinds of tests, what strategies they used to prepare, how much time they spent studying, and their grades. The sheets are organized by subject and attached to their notebooks (possibly on the inside cover). Students can fill out the first part of the sheet just after taking each test. When you hand the tests back, have students record their grades. Encourage them to monitor their performances, reflecting on the strategies they used to prepare for and take each test and gauging how these paid off. Encourage the students to look for patterns of cause and effect between their study strategies, the kinds of tests, and their performances. Discuss correlations between preparation strategies and grades. After a while, you may also ask them to predict their grades on certain tests and see whether they're right!

2. At the end of the lesson, pass out the "Preparing for Tests" handout for students to review.

Connections

Testing Lesson 5.5: Understanding Your Memory

Testing Lesson 5.10: Summarizing Testing Strategies—Writing a Testing Handbook

Follow-Up Activity

After the students have taken a test, ask them to review their homework assignments to see how many of the test questions they had previously answered in some form while doing the assignments. Were the test questions worded a little differently or did they appear in a different form—say, an essay instead of a table or diagram? Ask students to use this strategy of connecting homework to test questions to help them prepare for future tests. Perhaps it will work better for some subjects than for others.

LESSON 5.8 Troubleshooting During a Test

Central Themes

Knowing Self

Knowing Process

Synopsis

A brainstorm and discussion to help students anticipate and plan for problems while actually taking a test.

What To Do

1. A day or two before a planned test, ask students to think back to tests they have taken in the past and to brainstorm a list of all the problems they have encountered while testing.

2. Once you have the list on the board, ask the students to help categorize their responses under a few subheadings. "Physical," "emotional," "intellectual" (or "content-based"), and "situational" (or "place-related") will probably be the largest categories, although it's always safe to have a "miscellaneous" category as well.

3. Now take each category and talk with students about how to deal with these problems. Below are a few suggestions, but feel free to focus on the ideas your students come up with.

    *   *Emotional problems* (test anxiety, worry about a personal problem)
        Discuss with students the nature of test anxiety: the physical discomfort of muscle tension, upset stomach, and sweating, and the mental/emotional problems of worrying, not being able to think, "freezing," and so on. Assure them that these reactions are perfectly normal, even common. (Many adults still have nightmares about testing situations!) However, there are ways to deal with them and you will be discussing some of those ways in class.
        Role play stressful pre-test situations with the students. Have one student assume the teacher's role and give advice to an anxiety-ridden student played by the teacher.
        Role play a positive self-image and a positive, confident attitude toward tests with the students. Emphasize the following attitudes:

        *   Think about the test as an opportunity both to show what you know and to learn something about yourself.
        *   Tell yourself, "I can and will perform well on this test." See yourself as *in control of* your test performance.

- Remember that tests aren't perfect. Some are fairer and clearer than others. Simply do your best with the test before you.

Acknowledge the expertise of the skillful test takers in your class by having them discuss and demonstrate what they do to stay calm and clear-headed in a testing situation. (If necessary, add to their discussion the techniques of focusing, relaxing, and positive thinking.)

- *Physical problems* (of the "I was too hungry/tired to concentrate" variety)
  On the night before the test, eat and sleep as you normally do. Get your usual amount of sleep, relaxation, exercise, and food.
  If remembering to do this is a problem, use the buddy system. Have a friend call you and remind you about bedtime, or wake you up in time for breakfast.
- *Intellectual problems* (not understanding the questions, forgetting information, getting stumped)
  Ask questions (another role-playing opportunity here).
  Write immediately on the edge of your paper any facts/formulas you might forget.
  Skip hard questions (marking them so you'll know to come back—don't forget!).
- *Situational problems* (running out of time, not having notes or pencils)
  Check the time limit at the beginning and plan how much time to allot to each part.
  Pack your book bag the night before.

Connections

Writing Lesson 3.4: Getting Unstuck (for help with essay questions)

Homework Lesson 4.3: Personal Solutions to Homework Difficulties, Part C

Follow-Up Activity

The morning after a test, or certainly before the papers are handed back, have the students write down any problems they were coping with during the test: forgetting something they knew well, not being able to finish, feeling nervous, or anything that stood in the way of their performing the way they would have liked or thought they should have. Then ask them to write why they had that problem and what they think they can do to overcome it on the next test. Tell the students you would like them to share the information with you by passing in the papers so you can help them solve their problems. Suggest that it would be helpful to know if everyone was having a particular difficulty: Maybe there was really a problem with the test itself and you would need to know this in order to correct it. For instance, if no one completed the test, perhaps it was too long. For those students who don't wish to share their concerns, the writing exercise in itself should help their self-awareness. For you, the teacher, this process could save a long gripe session in class that could easily take more time than the journal entries would.

LESSON 5.9 After the Test

Central Theme

Reworking

Synopsis

An activity and discussion to show what can be learned from a careful review of graded tests.

What To Do

1. Remind students of the point introduced in Lesson 1 of this section—that tests are sources of information (like the pilot's altimeter reading). Explain that you're about to give them a test completed by a "mystery student" and that you'd like them to examine it for clues that will tell them what kind of a test-taker the student is. Distribute copies of a sample test that you have completed and graded. (It would be best if the test covered material familiar to the students.) It should contain various errors of the types made by the students in the class.

2. Discuss each mistake with the students. Note on the chalkboard the type of question the "student" missed. Ask the students to examine the mistake and to suggest why the test-taker may have had trouble with it. Carelessness? Misreading the question? Not understanding the directions? Not knowing the material?

3. Now make a list of the types of questions that the test-taker did especially well on.

4. Ask the students to find patterns in the lists. What kinds of questions were the hardest for this student? What kinds of questions did she answer best? What mistakes did she make most often?

5. What could this student do in the future to better prepare for tests?

6. If time permits, have students look at one of their own graded tests and ask them to analyze their performances just as they analyzed the mystery student's paper. If the test is one that they took after they began keeping their testing log (introduced in Lesson 7), encourage them to consult the log to see what kinds of strategies they used in preparing for the test.

7. What kinds of questions were hardest for them? What kinds were easy? What mistakes did they make most often? What might they do in the future to improve their performance? (Encourage them to recall strategies discussed in earlier lessons of this section.)

8. Ask several students to summarize how best to profit from a careful review of graded tests. Ask the students to name positive and negative aspects of a graded test. List the responses on the chalkboard. Review the kinds of information both teachers and students learn from graded tests.

Note

Students will best learn from graded tests when teachers go over tests in class immediately after handing them back. This gives students a chance to review, correct wrong answers, ask questions, and check the teacher's grading for errors (they love finding teacher errors!). If you go over tests regularly in class, consider requiring students to correct their answers. In addition, advise students to save tests or quizzes that they can use for review when preparing for later, more comprehensive tests.

Connections

Testing Lesson 5.10: Summarizing Testing Strategies—Writing a Testing Handbook

Follow-Up Activities

1. When students have made a substantial number of entries in their testing logs, begin reviewing the logs with them periodically. What subject-matter tests are they doing best/worst on? What sorts of preparations seem to give them the best boost? How could they do better in the areas where they are weak?

2. Consider adding a brief process-reflection question to each test that you give. It might ask students to predict how they've done on the test, or to name a strategy that they used to prepare for this test—and how well they think it worked.

LESSON 5.10
Summarizing Testing Strategies—Writing a Testing Handbook

Central Themes

Knowing Why

Knowing Self

Knowing Differences

Knowing Process

Reworking

Synopsis

A writing/illustrating activity to help students synthesize their understanding of testing.

What To Do

1. Prepare copies of the following handout (from the Student Handout section):

    *   "Preparing for Tests." This handout summarizes test preparation tools and strategies discussed so far. It can accompany this lesson or Lesson 7: Studying for an Upcoming Test.

2. Begin by jogging students' memories about the sorts of test-related topics you've covered in class. Brainstorm with them about all the different things they've learned about tests. Their contributions will probably range from the very concrete and personal (I study better for history tests if I try to make up test questions ahead of time) to the very general (Everyone takes tests in and out of school). Put them all on the chalkboard.

3. Stand back and admire with the students the great wealth of material they've generated. Point out that this is very important stuff on the board, and that it might be useful to have it all in one place. Suggest that they, as a class, create a handbook (Does anyone know what a handbook is?) for testing. It can include general points as well as more personal points. They might also consider making it a gift to a fifth-grade (or younger) class.

4. Work with your students to outline the broad topics to be covered in the book. They might begin this by trying to organize their brainstormed responses. If students have trouble with this, you can use the following suggestions to prompt them:

- Getting Ready: The Long Run
- Getting Ready: The Short Term
- Taking the Test
- After the Test Comes Back

5. Once they've established the basic outline, talk about design. Do they want to have very general tips? Or, maybe, sections that give more offbeat ideas? How can they make sure their handbook is readable from a fifth- or fourth-grade perspective? What sorts of things will make it easier—and more fun—for younger students to read? Encourage them to use illustrations and diagrams where appropriate.

6. Once they have decided on a basic design approach, divide them into groups, one for each section of the outline. (You might want to add a production managing group here—one that will be responsible for the cover pages, table of contents, and being sure that everyone works with the same sorts of materials when they start making their final copies. During step 6, this group can give critiques of other groups' work.) Talk with them a little bit about how to work in small groups most efficiently. You might want to assign roles within the group, such as recorder, leader, and spokesperson.

7. The first task is for each group to determine very specifically the tips their unit will include. Once they have done this, have each group's spokesperson make a presentation to the class and allow the rest of the class to make suggestions about how to revise the content. A less time-consuming way to accomplish this is to have each group write out their ideas and submit them to the group working to their right. That group reviews the outline and sends it back to the author group with written suggestions and criticisms.

8. Once the content is set, the groups should move on to design. Will they use computers? Will they hand-write their pages? What sorts of illustrations should they use? How should they divvy up these jobs? Have the groups produce mock-up illustrations and page layouts first, and use them in the same presentation-critique-revision process that went on in step 6.

9. Putting the book together and "publishing" it is the next task. You might want to coordinate this effort, or you might have a production-managing group handle the details. Be sure to display the finished product, whatever publication method you choose.

10. Once the students are finished and have a complete product in their hands, help them evaluate the process of creating it. What was easy? What was hard? Did they learn anything new about test-taking procedures as they worked with others? What would they do differently if they undertook a similar project in the future?

Note

"Preparing for Tests" (from the Student Handout section) may be distributed if not done earlier following Testing Lesson 5.7: Studying for an Upcoming Test.

Connections

Testing Lesson 5.9: After the Test

Homework Lesson 4.3: Personal Solutions to Homework Difficulties, Part A, Homework Fair

Follow-Up Activity

Check back with the students in a few months to see how useful the testing section has been to them in their own test preparations. Now that some time has passed, initiate a class discussion on the pros and cons of this project.

Student Handouts

For *Lesson 7: Studying for an Upcoming Test*
- Case Study of a Student Preparing for a Test
- The Test Log Sheet

For *Lesson 7: Studying for an Upcoming Test*, or

Lesson 10: Summarizing Testing Strategies—Writing a Testing Handbook
- Preparing for Tests

Case Study of a Student Preparing for a Test

Tom, a sixth-grader in Ms. Washington's introductory algebra class, has a math test on Friday. Ms. Washington announced the test on Monday, and Tom wrote it down in his notebook.

By Tuesday night, Tom was worried about the test. He didn't think he understood the material very well. He tried to do some extra problems, but grew frustrated and closed his book. He decided to watch TV before going to bed. "I have all Wednesday and Thursday to study anyway," he assured himself. "I need to relax now."

On Wednesday night, Tom grew more and more nervous about his test. He did all his other homework first, so that it was late by the time he got around to studying algebra. Tom realized that he was tired and couldn't concentrate very well. He quickly looked over the chapters and then went to bed. He said to himself, "I'll just do some problems tomorrow and then I hope I'll be able to get it. I'm too nervous and tired to work now."

On Thursday in class, Ms. Washington went over the material that would be on the test. When she asked if anyone had any questions, Tom thought to himself, "She'll think I'm stupid if I say that I'm having trouble with this stuff. I'll just figure it out myself tonight."

By Thursday night, Tom was panicked. He was so nervous that he had a hard time sitting still. He fidgeted with the pages of his textbook and tapped his pencil nervously on his desk. He tried to do some problems, but found he got stuck in the same place every time. Frustrated, he looked up the answers in the back of the book. Then he put his books away, saying, "Oh well. I'll bet nobody else understands this either. Maybe the test will be easy anyway. Yeah, I just have to hope it will be easy."

Test Log Sheet

Subject: English/Language Arts

Date of test	Kind of test	Preparation strategies	Time spent studying	Grade

Subject: Social Studies

Date of test	Kind of test	Preparation strategies	Time spent studying	Grade

Subject: Math

Date of test	Kind of test	Preparation strategies	Time spent studying	Grade

Subject: Science

Date of test	Kind of test	Preparation strategies	Time spent studying	Grade

Preparing for Tests

During Class

I. Listen in class.

II. Monitor myself.

    A. Am I paying attention?
    B. Am I staying on task?
    C. Do I understand? If not, ask for clarification!

III. Take good notes.

    A. Use key (most important) words and phrases.
    B. Write meanings in my own words.

In School and at Home

IV. Read material first for general understanding.

V. Re-read and highlight or take notes.

    A. Highlight to identify important phrases.
    B. Highlight on worksheets, workbooks that can be written in, and notes, but not school-owned textbooks.
    C. Take good notes.
       1. Use key words and phrases.
       2. Write meanings in my own words.
       3. Skip lines between topics.
       4. Use drawings or diagrams if appropriate.
       5. Use separate notebooks or sections for each subject. Label them.
       6. Rewrite sloppy notes.
       7. Notetaking is critical to success in school! My achievement often depends upon the quality of my notes.

VI. Check my understanding of the material.

VII. Review the material several times before the test.

    A. Use memorizing techniques (mnemonics).
       1. Repetition or rehearsal.
       2. Clustering words by category.
       3. Word interactions.
       4. Method of loci (places).
       5. Acronyms (words in which each letter is the first letter of another word).
       6. Acrostics (similar to acronyms, but use first letters in sentences, not words).
    B. Re-read notes.
    C. Consider the kind of test (multiple choice? short answer?) I have to take and the subject (math? social studies?). Pay special attention to tests and subjects where I don't usually do as well.
    D. Practice, practice, practice! Work on problems, sentences, definitions, examples, and exercises. Check that my answers are correct.
    E. Don't wait until the night before to start studying!

VIII. Summarize the material in my own words for practice.

Index

Entries followed by an H indicate student handouts.